The Rugby League G

By Peter Lush and Dave Farrar

Hull F.C. versus Halifax Blue Sox - August 2000

LONDON LEAGUE PUBLICATIONS Ltd.

The Rugby League Grounds Guide

© Copyright Peter Lush and Dave Farrar

The moral right of Peter Lush and Dave Farrar to be identified as the authors has been asserted. Foreword © David Hinchliffe M.P.

Photographs by Peter Lush except where indicated and may not be reproduced without permission. Contact London League Publications to order prints. All photos copyright to the photographer.

Front cover photos: St Helens vs. Melbourne Storm Jan 2000 at the JJB Stadium, Wigan; Leigh supporters at the 2000 NFP Grand Final at Swinton; and The Valley - London Broncos versus. Wigan June 2000

Back cover photos: Green Monster at Hull, August 2000; Food on the Move - catering at Dewsbury, January 2000; Melbourne Storm supporters at St Helens versus Melbourne Storm January 2000 at the JJB Stadium, Wigan

A CIP catalogue record for this book is available from the British Library.

First published in Great Britain in April 2001 by:
London League Publications Ltd., P.O. Box 10441, London E14 0SB

ISBN: 1-903659-02-7

Cover design by: Stephen McCarthy Graphic Design
                          46, Clarence Road London N15 5BB

Printed and bound by: Catford Print Centre, PO Box 563, Catford,
                          London SE6 4PY

Foreword

I was delighted to be asked to write the Foreword to this important book. Its timely publication will be welcomed by the many fans of our great game who value their regular visits to "away" grounds and the opportunity to widen their experience of Rugby League's rich heritage.

Visiting various members of the Rugby League family has to me always had parallels with childhood visits to one relative or another. I seemed to grow up with "visiting", being trailed almost every week-end to see uncles, aunts and cousins all over the place.

On one side of the family, they lived in very humble abodes, in terraces or on council estates; on the other, in more substantial private houses with frilly tablecloths on which we had the ham teas I remember so well

"Visiting" took on another meaning when I got to around 12. By then, I had watched the great Wakefield Trinity side of the late fifties and early sixties for several years but only ever at our home ground of Belle Vue. I had heard mention of faraway places like Post Office Road and Central Park and once caught a magic glimpse of Fartown on match day when going for a Saturday lunch at my parents' friends in Huddersfield.

I'll never forget looking down at that ground where a packed crowd roared on the likes of Valentine and Ramsden and wishing like hell I could be there.

I am not sure of the exact year but I know for a fact that it was a Boxing Day when, with permission from my mother, I boarded the Trinity supporters' bus in Wakefield to take the ten mile journey to Headingley for the match with Leeds. Before the advent of Super League turned the world upside down, the Boxing Day Derby between these two great sides was one of the season's highlights and this young lad's eager anticipation of seeing the likes of Harold Poynton facing Lewis Jones was accompanied by the great excitement of visiting an away ground for the very first time.

Sadly, I had a long wait to achieve the status of visiting supporter as the match was called off because of fog. As our bus pulled in to the car park behind Headingley's South Stand, it was a real sickener learning that we would be turning round and heading straight back to Wakefield.

But by the time I was in my late teens, I could boast of having travelled to virtually every professional Rugby League ground in the country. I have rich memories of seemingly endless journeys to places like Barrow; of being awakened by passing churchgoers after spending the night in the back of a van in Ambleside's churchyard between watching Castleford's Challenge Cup match at Whitehaven on the Saturday and Trinity's match at Salford on the Sunday; of inevitable pre M62 stops at the Floating Light pub high up on the wrong side of the Pennines

And like the homes of childhood relatives, the grounds I visited varied from the very modest to the more substantial. They varied in their location, their characteristics, their decor, their atmosphere and had their own very individual smells. Having grown up on Belle Vue's unique aroma of steam loco sheds, coal fired power station and wintergreen, I experienced a rich and varied bouquet ranging from fish docks to chemical works and frying fast food.

Some of those relatives moved from back to backs with outside loos to spanking brand new semis on posh estates, but they weren't necessarily happier as a result. I reflected on this particular point as I saw Fartown dismantled and more recently Central Park bulldozed to the ground. We have to move with the times but the Thrum Halls of this world had qualities and history that can never be replicated elsewhere.

I can no longer claim familiarity with all of our games' grounds because so many clubs have moved to pastures new. It is therefore a pleasure to read this much needed comprehensive and up to date guide to the game's modern grounds. It's authors - Peter Lush and Dave Farrar - must rank among domestic Rugby League's most travelled followers and they have done a great service by putting together this excellent publication.

David Hinchliffe M.P.

David Hinchliffe is the M.P. for Wakefield and a life-long Wakefield Trinity supporter. He is the Secretary of the All-Party Parliamentary Rugby League Group and the author of *Rugby's Class War*.

Preface

One of the great problems facing Rugby League, as with other sports, is how to modernise its stadiums and facilities, while not destroying tradition and history associated with them. Since we last published a grounds guide in 1996, Central Park is now part of history, as are Watersheddings and Thrum Hall. At the time of writing, Knowsley Road is in its last season, Warrington are planning to move from Wilderspool, and the Bradford Bulls have moved across the city to Valley Parade while Odsal is redeveloped.

But there are also positive aspects to new stadiums for the sport. The completed Alfred McAlpine Stadium in Huddersfield is now one of the sport's key venues, and has become a regular venue for Challenge Cup semi-finals and World Cup matches. In Widnes, Naughton Park has become the Autoquest Stadium, a very modern multi-sport arena. And while the JJB Stadium and The Shay may not yet feel like home for Wigan and Halifax supporters respectively, they do offer better facilities than either of the old stadiums ever did. New supporters attracted to the game will expect seats under cover, decent food facilities and proper areas for people with disabilities, something too many Rugby League grounds in the past lacked. And since our last book, Hunslet have a permanent home in south Leeds.

Another development over the past five years has been ground sharing, primarily with football clubs. Along with Wigan, Halifax and Huddersfield, Chorley, Doncaster, the London Broncos, Oldham, Rochdale and Swinton all share grounds with football clubs. In most cases, these arrangements have seen better facilities developed for supporters. And in a some cases, ground sharing with rugby union clubs has started, or is a realistic prospect.

The lowering of rugby's Berlin Wall in 1995 has also seen major Rugby League matches played at Twickenham, Murrayfield and the Millennium Stadium. Although some supporters still, understandably, have reservations about any of "our money" going into union's coffers, it has allowed us to visit these stadiums and watch a proper game of rugby, even if the heavens seemed to open on every occasion in the 2000 Rugby League World Cup.

Whatever level you watch the game at, we hope you find this book useful. Despite over 15,000 miles of driving to compile it, we enjoyed producing it, and were fortunate to see entertaining matches most of the time.

Peter Lush and Dave Farrar

About the authors

Peter Lush was introduced to Rugby League by Dave Farrar in October 1980, when having nothing better to do on a Sunday afternoon, he went to watch Fulham play York at Craven Cottage. 20 years later he is still enthusiastic about the game. He also has a season ticket for West Ham United FC, has a soft spot for Brentford FC, and is a member of Middlesex County Cricket Club. Apart from the books listed below, he also co-wrote *The Employment Handbook - a guide for housing co-operatives*. He wrote regularly for *London Calling!*, still contributes occasionally to *The Greatest Game* and once wrote a match report for *League Express*. When not writing about or watching sport, he works as a housing and personnel consultant. He has developed an intimate knowledge of the M62, A1, M11, M1 and M6 while working on this book.

Dave Farrar has been watching Rugby League for nearly 40 years. He was born in Salford and his parents watched the original Red Devils (Salford RLFC) in the 1930s. He moved to London in 1980 and started watching Fulham. He has now followed Rugby League in London for 20 years and is a committed supporter of the London Broncos. Apart from the books listed below, he has also written *The Right to Vote* (with Yve Amor). He also wrote regularly for *London Calling!* and is vice-chairman of the London Broncos supporters club. He works as a manager in local government.

Previous publications:
From Fulham to Wembley- 20 years of professional Rugby League in London
edited by Dave Farrar and Peter Lush
Touch and Go - A History of Professional Rugby League in London
by Dave Farrar and Peter Lush with Michael O'Hare
I Wouldn't Start from Here by Peter Lush and Dave Farrar
The Sin Bin by Steve Spencer, Peter Hardy and Dave Farrar
From Arundel to Zimbabwe by Robin Osmond, Peter Lush and Dave Farrar
Tries in the Valleys edited by Peter Lush and Dave Farrar
Going to the Cricket by Robin Osmond and Peter Lush
Our Game edited by Peter Lush and Dave Farrar

Thank You

We would like to thank all the club officials who provided information for the book, helped arranged photographer's passes and were often very hospitable. We would also like to thank Trevor Delaney for permission to use material from *The Grounds of Rugby League* and *The International Grounds of Rugby League* for the ground histories; Steve McCarthy for providing most of the maps; Al Ferrier for his checking and information gathering; Peter Cross for surveying several grounds for us; Harry Edgar for doing the survey of Whitehaven; Andrew Quirke for doing the survey of St Helens; John Drake for permission to use material from the rugbytreize.com website; Ian Cooper for permission to use information from the BARLA handbook; Julian Harrison for providing information about the Rugby League Conference and Sandra for help with the tourist information. Naturally, any mistakes that sneaked in are our responsibility.

How to use this book

Road travel: We recommend using a standard road map with this book. The sketch maps are not to scale, and only cover immediately by the grounds.

Facilities: The facilities provided at grounds may vary depending on the match and crowd expected. If a particular facility is important for you, we would recommend checking in advance.

Facilities for people with disabilities: Some facilities need to be booked in advance. We would recommend phoning in advance to check - especially if visiting a ground for the first time.

Clubcall and other information lines: Calls charged at premium rates.

There are bound to be mistakes in the book. From January 2000 to February 2001 we visited every professional Rugby League ground in England, but there can be changes that we are not aware of at the time of production. Please let us know any mistakes you find, so that we can make corrections in future editions. Please send comments or corrections to: London League Publications Ltd, P.O. Box 10441, London E14 0SB.

Please note that the authors and London League Publications Ltd do not accept any liability for any loss, injury or inconvenience sustained by people as a result of using the information or advice in this book.

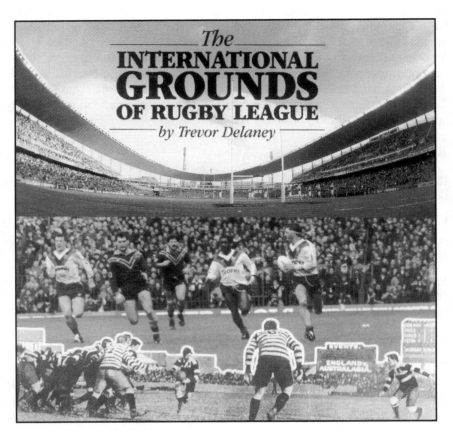

The
INTERNATIONAL
GROUNDS
OF RUGBY LEAGUE
by Trevor Delaney

Published in 1995, *The International Grounds of Rugby League* covers the history and development of every stadium in the world, which staged rugby league internationals during the game's first century. Lavishly illustrated with over 200 photographs, many in full colour.

Originally priced at £12.95, it is available from the author/publisher at 11 Gledhill Road, Bradford BD3 9LX for **only** £4 (which includes postage and packing). Cheques payable to T. Delaney.

Contents

British professional clubs

JOIN THE
Rugby League
Supporters
Association

And get The Greatest Game! delivered free
Don't just read the headlines... Join the RLSA and help us make them

Our aims:

- To democratically represent the views of our members
- To campaign for supporters' views to be heard at all levels in the game
- To encourage friendship between supporters of all clubs and countries
- To seek to work for the promotion and expansion of rugby league

To join the RLSA, and get TGG! delivered to your door, just complete the following details and send with your payment to the address below. Please make cheques payable to the RLSA.

Yes! I would like to join the RLSA and receive my four issues of TGG! starting from issue no____
I enclose a cheque / postal order for £6.00

Name:

Address: (Please include your postcode)

Optional information:
Telephone (including STD code)
Email
I follow...
(Please enter your team or tick one of the boxes)   [] The Super League []
The Northern Ford Premiership [] Other
N.B. The RLSA does not release member details to third parties
Post to: RLSA Memberships, 210, Calverley Lane, Leeds LS13 1AG
(photocopy if you do not want to cut the book)

Barrow Border Raiders

Ground: Craven Park
Address: Craven Park, Duke Street, Barrow in Furness LA14 5UW
Office address: 78, Scott Street, Barrow in Furness LA14 1QE
Telephone: 01229-830470 (ground), 01229-820273 and
01229-824454 (office)
Fax: 01229-820273
Website: www.barrowraiders.com
E-mail: barrowrlfc@themail.co.uk ; Shop: goldrush@rugbyshop.fsnet.co.uk
Capacity: 6,047
Number of seats: 1,000

History of ground: Craven Park is now 70 years old and has a record attendance of 21,651 for a league game against Salford in 1938. Barrow previously played at Cavendish Park from 1875 to 1914, the Parade Ground, from 1875 to1880, and Little Park, Roose from 1914 to 1931, when the club moved to Craven Park.

The present ground cost £7,500 when originally built, which included £2,500 for the site. Floodlights were installed in 1966 and first used for the visit of St Helens. In the 2000 World Cup the Fiji versus Russia game was held at the ground. A club legend was honoured when the new stand, opened in April 1999, was named after former player Willie Horne, who died in March 2001. He played for the club from 1942 to 1959 at stand off, and won every honour in the game, including captaining Great Britain.

Description of ground: One of the game's historic venues. The new Willie Horne stand provides seating under cover with good views, with the rest of the ground being terracing, mainly under cover. It is well maintained, but apart from the new stand there has been little modernisation. Adequate for the club's present crowds, but would need some modernisation should the club seek Super League status.

Stands and terraces:
Restrictions on use: None
Views from different areas: Slight obstruction by pillars in stand, and in corners of back rows. Views from terracing good, although pillars would cause an obstruction in a large crowd.

1

Under cover: Stand and most of terracing.
Transfers to seats: In ground.

Entrance price reductions:

Children: Yes

Disabled: No

Senior citizens: Yes

Family tickets or reductions: Yes

Students: No

Club shop:
At club office in town, and at club on match days, near main entrance.
Opening hours: Office hours at club office, match days at ground.
Main items of stock: Shirts, fleeces, hats, ties, scarves, badges, mugs, souvenirs, some books.

Supporters with disabilities:
Wheelchair access or designated area: In front of stand.
Other special facilities: None.
Disabled toilets: In players' tunnel.
Access to facilities (bars etc.): In stand, but not on terracing.
Designated car parking at ground: No.

Catering:
Snack bars on terracing and in stand.
Main items on sale: Burgers, pies, tea and coffee, cold drinks, crisps, confectionery.
Restaurant at ground: No.

Bars:
On terracing in corner opposite main stand. Members only, but guests can sign in - no charge.

Facilities for activities for junior supporters: None.
Match-day creche: No.
General facilities for hire: None.
Other sports at stadium: None
Local facilities, pubs, cafes or restaurants: Two pubs near ground in Duke Street, and Wheatsheaf Hotel in Anson Street.

Car parking:
No parking at ground.
Street parking: Adequate in immediate area. Restricted immediately around ground.

Public transport:
Station: Barrow (Abbey Road). Very limited Sunday service. From Station Approach turn left into Holker Street, right into Abbey Road, turn right at Ramsden Square into Duke Street and ground is on left.
Buses: Most stop at the Town Hall, a few minutes walk from the ground, including 1, 1a, 2, 5, 6, 7. Walk down Duke Street, cross Ramsden Square and ground is on left.

Directions by car:
From M6: Junction 36, and follow A590 direct to Barrow. Turn left into Duke Street, and ground is on right.
N.B. Although most of this road is dual carriageway, it can be very busy in the summer. Allow at least one and a half hours from the M6 in summer. Grange over Sands is a nice place to stop for a meal on the way, about 2 miles off the A590.

Tourist Information:
Forum 28, Duke Street, Barrow in Furness, Cumbria, LA14 1HU.
Tel: 01229-894784.
Fax: 01229-894703.

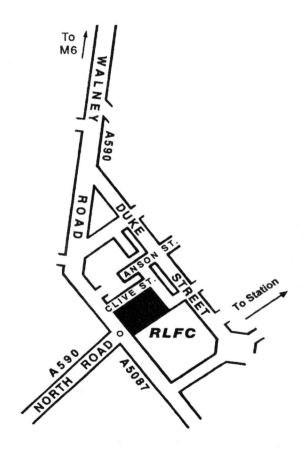

3

BARROW BORDER RAIDERS SOUVENIR SHOP PRICE LIST

78 Scott Street, Barrow-in-Furness Cumbria LA14 1QE
Tel. 01229 824454. Fax. 01229 820273
E-mail: goldrush@rugbyshop.fsnet.co.uk

REPLICA SHIRTS AND CLOTHING

Shirts: Home (Blue and White) - Away (Red and White)

Adult - Small, Med, Large, XLarge & XXLarge	£38.00
Child - 26/28", 28/30", 30/32"	£32.00
Fleece Tops (Navy Blue) Med, Large, Xlarge, XXlarge (Half zip)	£35.00
V-Neck Fleece Tops (Navy Blue - sizes as above)	£30.00
Lambswool & acrylic jumpers (with club badge) in various colours (40" - 48")	£25.00
Showerproof Windbreakers (Navy/Red) Sizes Medium, Large, Xlarge and XXLarge	£30.00
Polo Shirts in Black and Navy - Sizes Med, Large, Xlarge	£18.00

OTHER ITEMS

Club Ties	£8.00
Scarves	£5.00
Raiders China Mugs	£3.50
Bronx Hats	£6.99
Baseball Caps	£7.99
Twin Towers - The story of Barrow's R.L. Challenge Cup Finals	£14.99
Willie Horne Grandstand Metal Badges	£2.50
Other Barrow Metal Badges - various designs	£2.50

Add £1 postage on all items

Do you require any old Barrow Rugby League programmes for your collection? Ring John Spoor on the above number.

For details of the Barrow Border Raiders Rugby Gold Rush, phone 01229-824454 or contact the club office.

4

Batley Bulldogs

Ground: Mount Pleasant.
Address: Challenge Family Stand, Heritage Road, Mount Pleasant, Batley, WF17 7NZ.
Telephone: 01924-470062
Fax: 01924-470062
Website: None
E-mail: None
Capacity: 5,000.
Number of seats: 650.

History of ground: Mount Pleasant is one of the most atmospheric grounds in Rugby League. The first game was way back in 1880 when the Gallant Youths played Bradford Zingari. The infamous slope is a memorable feature of the ground, as is its hilltop vista from which you can see Emley Moor. The record attendance was 23,989 for the visit of Leeds for a third round Challenge Cup game in 1925. Mount Pleasant is with Belle Vue, Wakefield, one of the oldest Rugby League grounds in the world, and the club celebrated their centenary at their match against Fulham in 1981 with a famous victory against the League's new London team.

Description of ground: The ground has undergone a major modernisation programme in the last 10 years and is now fine for Northern Ford Premiership matches. The Family Stand, a covered terraced area, is at the Heritage Road end of the ground, and also houses the club offices. On the south side of the ground is the 650 seat Heritage stand. Opposite this is the Long Stand, an uncovered terrace, which the club are planning to replace at the end of the 2001 season. The area behind the far goal is currently (Spring 2001) being developed. The completion of the planned development works will give a 10,000 capacity.

The ground is very high, which provides stunning views. One terrace by the Heritage Stand is named after former Batley player, Roy Powell.

Stands and terraces:
Restrictions on use: None.
Views from different areas: Restricted view from back two rows of the Heritage Stand.

Under cover: Family Stand and Heritage Stand.
Transfers to seats: No transfers within the ground. Use entrance 1 for the Heritage Stand.

Entrance price reductions:

Children: Yes.

Senior citizens: Yes.

Students: Half price season ticket.

Disabled: Carer scheme - carer free.

Family tickets or reductions: No.

Club shop:

Behind the Heritage Stand.

Opening hours: Match days.

Main items of stock: A few videos and shirts, souvenirs, old programmes. Also sells tea, coffee and sweets.

Supporters with disabilities:

Wheelchair access or designated area: Ramp into middle section of Heritage Stand. Elevated view and some protection from bad weather. Also designated places in Challenge Family Stand.

Other special facilities: None.

Disabled toilets: Behind Heritage Stand and beside the players entrance in the Challenge Family Stand.

Access to facilities (bars etc.): At back of Heritage Stand. Extended pathways around ground for easy wheelchair access

Designated car parking at ground: No.

Catering:

Burger bars at corner Long Stand & Family Stand & behind Heritage Stand.

Main items on sale: Burgers, tea & coffee, etc.

Restaurant at ground: No.

Bars:

Underneath Heritage Stand (due for completion spring 2001). Batley Taverners Club - outside ground by main entrance.

Facilities for activities for junior supporters: 13 junior teams run by Batley Boys Club, 6 dressing rooms in Family Challenge Stand with all weather training pitch and floodlights.

Match-day creche: None.

General facilities for hire: Taverners Club.

Other sports at stadium: Next door to Batley Cricket Club. Bowls green behind Taverners Club.

Local facilities, pubs, cafes or restaurants: White Hart on Wellington Street and Wilton Arms on Commercial Street both serve Sunday lunch.

Car parking:
Adequate parking at ground.
Street parking: Taylor Street - residents only. Some street parking near ground.

Public transport:
Information: 0113-245-7676.
Nearest station: Batley. From train station: turn sharp left down Back Station Road, past roundabout and down Alexandra Road. Turn right at the bottom onto Bradford Road, then first left up Taylor Street. Turn left at the top into Purwell Hall Road, then first left into Heritage Road.
Buses: 251,252   (Along Bradford Road - no buses go direct to Mount Pleasant)
The walk from the bus or train station is ¾ mile, and involves a steep climb, particularly up Taylor Street - allow extra time.
From bus station: walk up Branch Road (away from main road - Bradford Road), across Market Square, into Cambridge Street. At the junction turn left into Wellington Street and first right up Victoria Avenue. Continue up Purwell Hall Road, then turn left into Heritage Road.

Directions by car: *From west:* Take junction 25 on M62. Take A644 signposted Brighouse, then left onto A62 (Leeds), then turn right onto A644. Take A644 to Dewsbury, follow signs on ring road for Bradford A652. Take A652 to Batley, turn left into Taylor Street. Turn left at top of road for Mount Pleasant complex.
From east: Take junction 27 on M62. Take A62 signposted Huddersfield. Turn left onto A652, then right into Taylor Street, then as above.
From south: Take junction 40 on M1, A638 to Dewsbury (not sign to Batley), then as above from west when in Dewsbury.

Tourist Information:
Yorkshire Mill Village TIC, Bradford Road, Batley WF17 5LZ.
Tel: 01924-426670. Fax: 01924-446096

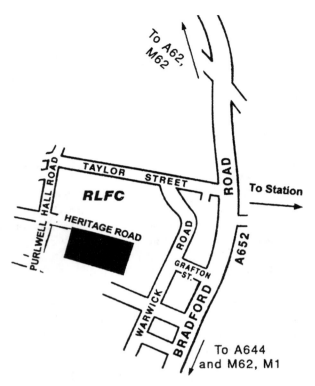

The Heritage Stand

Bradford Bulls

Ground: Odsal Stadium (for 2001 and 2002 - Valley Parade).
Address: Odsal Stadium, Bradford, West Yorkshire, BD6 1BS.
Match ground address: Bradford City F.C., Valley Parade, Bradford, W. Yorkshire, BD8 7DY.
Telephone: 01274-733899
Fax: 01274-724730
Website: www.bradfordbulls.co.uk
E-mail: info@bradfordbulls.co.uk

History of ground: Odsal is famous throughout Rugby League and has proved to be an ideal venue for summer Rugby League. It was equally famous for its own micro-climate in the old days of winter Rugby League. The old bowl has been used for other sports such as speedway (including staging World Finals) and top flight soccer. Its huge capacity was tested to the full in 1954 for the Challenge Cup replay between Warrington and Halifax when an official figure of 102,569 squeezed into the ground. Robert Gate's book *There Were a lot More There Than That* puts the actual attendance even higher. This official attendance was a world record until beaten in 2000 by Stadium Australia. In September 1999, a record attendance for a Super League match was set when 24,020 saw the Bulls play Leeds.

Odsal was opened in 1934 and hosted a Bradford Northern record crowd of 69,429 for a third round Challenge Cup against Huddersfield in 1953. Bradford had previously played at Bradford Park Avenue (as Bradford) and as Bradford Northern at Greenfield Athletic Ground (1907/8), Birch Lane (1908-1934). Bradford have also played games at Valley Parade (the home of Bradford City FC). Floodlights were first used in 1951 for a tour match against New Zealand in front of 29,072 supporters, but were beyond repair by 1960. New floodlights were inaugurated in 1979 for the visit of St Helens. The ground hosted nine Championship finals between 1957 and 1973 and eleven test matches between 1947 and 1980.

The information provided below is for Valley Parade.

Description of ground:
Valley Parade has undergone considerable modernisation and development over recent years to be able to cope with the demands of Premiership football. It is now an all-seater stadium with a capacity of just over 18,000.

Stands and terraces:
All seat stadium with all areas under cover.

Entrance price reductions:

Children: Yes.

Senior citizens: Yes.

Students: Yes.

Disabled: Contact club for details.

Family tickets or reductions: Contact club for details.

Club shop:
Main items of stock: Souvenirs, shirts etc. Apart from the shop at Odsal, there is also the Bulls on Broadway, city centre superstore on Broadway, opposite C&A, and The Bull Pen at Morrisons Supermarket in the Victoria Shopping Centre in Girlington.

Supporters with disabilities:
Wheelchair access or designated area: Places in CIBA stand and Sunwin stand.
Other special facilities: None.
Disabled toilets: Near wheelchair areas.
Access to facilities (bars etc.): Contact club for details.
Designated car parking at ground: Contact club for details.

Catering:
Kiosks in all areas of the ground.
Restaurant at ground: No.

Bars:
On main concourse.

Facilities for activities for junior supporters: Odsal was excellent for match day activities. These will continue at Valley Parade.
Match-day creche: None.
General facilities for hire: Contact Bradford City F.C.

Other sports at stadium: Football (Bradford City F.C.)
Local facilities: Many pubs and cafes in local area.

Car parking:
None at ground.
Street parking: Limited, with some streets being residents only. Some places on Midland Road.

Public transport:
Information: 0113-245-7676
Stations: Bradford Forster Square is ¾ mile from the ground. Turn right into Manor Row, then at ring road either Manningham Lane (turn right into Valley Parade) or Midland Road lead to the ground.
Bradford Interchange is 1¼ miles from the ground.
Buses: Numerous from stand B12 in the Interchange to ground.

Directions by car:
Take the ring road (A6177) towards the north of the city and turn into Manningham Lane (A650) or Midland Road. From the city centre, the A650 from the inner ring road (A6181)

Tourist information:
Central Library
Princes Way,
Bradford,
W. Yorkshire
BD1 1NN.
Tel: 01274 - 753678.
Fax: 01274-739067.

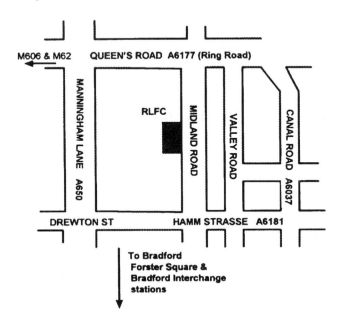

Castleford Tigers

Ground: The Jungle (formerly known as Wheldon Road).
Address: The Jungle, Wheldon Road, Castleford, WF10 2SD.
Telephone: 01977 552674. Merchandise and lottery: 01977-555703
Fax: 01977 518007.
Website: www.castigers.com
E-mail: info@castigers.com
Capacity: 11,750
Number of seats: 1,500

History of ground:
Wheldon Road is a compact stadium which provides a cosy Super League venue. The first competitive game league was held in 1926 for Castleford's game against St Helen's Recs in a Challenge Cup tie, when the club were still a junior side. The ground had originally been the home of Castleford Town FC who went under after being refused entry into the Third Division. Castleford previously played at "Sandy Desert", Lock Lane in 1926-7.

The record attendance for the ground is 25,449 for a third round Challenge Cup game against Hunslet in 1935. However, the second round Challenge Cup game against Hull KR in 1967 was reported to have been more, the official attendance was 22,582, plus an estimated 8,000 getting in without paying. This total attendance was somewhat greater than the town's population. Castleford installed floodlights in the 1965-6 season, and celebrated by winning the BBC2 Floodlit Trophy, which the club held for the next two seasons.

Description of ground: A traditional Rugby League ground, with a relatively small number of seats, covered terracing behind one goal and on one side and open terracing otherwise. New sponsorship, new marketing and community work developments, combined with more success on the pitch have given the Tigers a new lease of life. While the ground is clearly in need of development to meet the standards of a modern stadium, it has a far more lively feel to it than in the past. Facilities for children have been provided behind the main stand and on our visit there was a steel band playing in a marquee and clowns to provide more pre-match entertainment. The Tigers now seem to have got to grips with summer rugby and Super League and are making a success of it.

Stands and terraces:
Restrictions on use: Limited number of seats for big games.
Views from different areas: Pillars on all three stands.
Under cover: One end uncovered and small areas at side of stand.
Transfers to seats: Pay at turnstiles

Entrance price reductions:
Children: Yes, up to age sixteen.
Senior citizens: Yes.
Students: Must be pre-purchased and college identification needed, both to purchase ticket and for match day.

Disabled: Yes (Wheelchair or blind only).
Family tickets or reductions: Family tickets available - must be pre-purchased.

Club shop:
By main entrance in Wheldon Road. Also in Carlton Lanes shopping centre.
Opening hours: Office hours and matchdays.
Main items of stock: Good selection of shirts and other clothing.

Supporters with disabilities:
Wheelchair access or designated area: Small area by main stand.
Other special facilities: None.
Disabled toilets: Contact club for information.
Access to facilities (bars etc.): At ground level.
Designated car parking at ground: Contact club.

Catering:
Burger bars and van behind main stand. Burger bars on covered terracing. Marquee behind main stand.
Main items on sale: Burgers, hot dogs, hot beef sandwiches, pie and peas.
Restaurant at ground: Yes.

Bars:
In main stand, marquee and beneath restaurant. No restrictions on use.

Facilities for activities for junior supporters: Bouncy castle, face painting, mascots, entertainers etc behind main stand

Match-day creche: None

General facilities for hire: None

Other sports at stadium: None

Local facilities, pubs, cafes or restaurants:

The Wheldale opposite the ground; The Early Bath – home of Lock Lane ARLFC on Wheldon Road. Other pubs on Wheldon Road near town centre.

Car parking:

Limited parking at ground.

Street parking: Some near ground.

Public transport:

Information: 0113-245-7676.

Nearest station: Castleford. ¾ mile walk to ground. From station follow Station Road to Aire St. Turn right and at roundabout straight across into Wheldon Rd.

Buses: 167, 168, 468. West Riding Buses depot is a few minutes walk from the ground on Wheldon Road.

Directions by car: Ground is well signposted from town centre

From west: M62 take junction 31, A655 to Castleford. At roundabout turn right into A6032 (Aire Street). At next roundabout, take second exit, which is Wheldon Road. Ground is on right.

From east: M62 take junction 32, A639 to Castleford. Turn right onto A656, at roundabout with A6032, turn right into Wheldon Road. Ground on right.

From north and south: Either A1, then M62 as for *east* above, or take B6136 from A1, which joins A639. Turn right, then as for *east* above.

Tourist Information:

Wakefield Tourist Information, Town Hall, Wood Street, Wakefield, W. Yorkshire WF1 2HQ.

Tel: 01924-295000/1. Fax: 01924-295283.

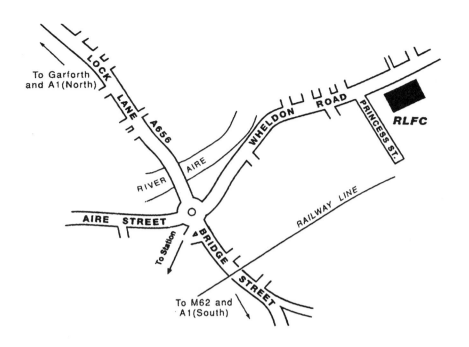

Castleford Tigers club shop

Chorley Lynx

Ground: Victory Park
Address: Victory Park, Duke Street, Chorley, Lancs PR7 3DU.
Telephone: 01257-263406
Fax: 01257-241625
Website: None
E-mail: None
Capacity: 5,000
Number of seats: 900

History of ground: Victory Park is a pleasant ground which is shared with non-league football club Chorley FC. The Chorley Rugby League team played their first game at the ground in 1989 against Trafford Borough in the Lancashire Cup, in front of 628 spectators. The Rugby League ground record attendance is 2,851 for the visit of Oldham in January 1990. Chorley have also played at Deepdale, the home of Preston North End FC. Floodlights were first used at Victory Park for a football match against the Tom Finney All Stars game in 1961.

Description of ground: A neat, well maintained ground. There is a wooden stand on one side, with terraces in front of it, and the disabled area. There is covered terracing behind both goals, and terraces or grass banks elsewhere. Adequate for the club's present needs.

Stands and terraces:
Restrictions on use: None.
Views from different areas: Good. Some minor obstruction from pillars. Some obstruction in back row seats in corners of stand.
Under cover: Stand and some terracing.
Transfers to seats: No charge for seats.

Entrance price reductions:
Children: Yes (under 16).   *Disabled:* No.
Senior citizens: Yes.   *Family tickets or reductions:* No.
Students: No.

Club shop:
Small cabin in ground, not open at present.
Opening hours: Not open at present.
Main items of stock: Contact club for souvenirs etc.

Supporters with disabilities:
Wheelchair access or designated area: In front of stand. Easy access to ground.
Other special facilities: None
Disabled toilets: Near scoreboard in corner of ground
Access to facilities (bars etc.): Snack room is accessible. Not to social club
Designated car parking at ground: No.

Catering:
Snack room and van inside ground.
Main items on sale: Burgers, pies, chips, tea & coffee, soup and confectionery in snack room. Burgers, tea & coffee from van.
Restaurant at ground: No

Bars:
Social club inside ground near entrance. No restrictions on use.

Facilities for activities for junior supporters: None
Match-day creche: None
General facilities for hire: Social club
Other sports at stadium: Football (Chorley F.C.)
Local facilities, pubs, cafes or restaurants: None in immediate area

Car parking:
Small car park at ground - no public access.
Street parking: No restrictions. Adequate for most matches.

Public transport:
Information: 0870-6082608
Nearest station: Chorley. A ½ mile walk to the ground. Turn left along Shepherds Way (A6). At the third roundabout (Bolton Street), bear left down Duke Street and turn left into Ashby Street.
Buses: Local buses stop on Bolton Rd. From bus station: ¾ mile walk to ground. Turn left uphill along Union St, and left at traffic lights into Bolton St. Just before the next roundabout, turn right into Duke Street, then left into Ashby Street.

Directions by car:

From east: M62 junction 14 M61 north. Junction 6 take A6 to Chorley. Turn left into Duke Street, just after roundabout with Bolton Street and A6, and left into Ashby Street.

From west and south: M6 take junction 27, A5029 towards Wigan. At junction with A49, go straight across onto B5239. Turn left onto A5106, and left onto A6. Then as above.

From north: M6 junction 30 take M61 south. Junction 8 take A6 south, turn right at roundabout into Bolton Street, then immediately left into Duke Street, than as above.

Tourist Information:

Bolton Tourist Information Centre, Town Hall, Victoria Square, Bolton, Lancs, BL1 1RU.
Tel.: 01204-334400. Fax: 01204-398101.
Email: tic@bolton-metro.demon.co.uk .

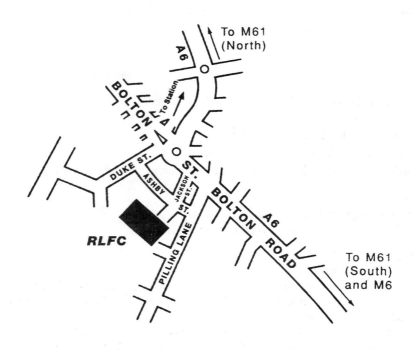

Dewsbury Rams

Ground: Ram Stadium
Address: Ram Stadium, Owl Lane, Dewsbury, W. Yorkshire, WF12 7RH.
Telephone: 01924-465489
Fax: 01924-437201
Website: www.dewsburyrams.com
E-mail: None
Capacity: 4,000
Number of seats: 1,000 (approx.)

History of ground: Dewsbury previously played at Crown Flatt which was their home from 1876. They had previously played at Sugar Lane as Dewsbury Athletic in 1875. The record attendance at Crown Flatt was 26,584 for a second round Yorkshire Cup replay against Halifax. The club moved out of Crown Flatt in 1991 due to it failing to meet minimum ground safety requirements, and moved into the newly built Owl Lane in 1994, following a period sharing with near neighbours Batley.

Description of ground: Modern J.D. Matthewman stand on the north side, with covered terracing on the south side. Grassed areas behind both goals. Fine for the Northern Ford Premiership, but would need further development to stage Super League matches.

Stands and terraces:
Restrictions on use: None.
Views from different areas: Good. Four pillars in J.D. Matthewman stand.
Under cover: Stand (front four rows not fully under cover) and terracing.
Transfers to seats: No transfers inside ground.

Entrance price reductions:
Children: Yes.
Senior citizens: Yes.
Students: No.
Disabled: Yes.

Family tickets or reductions: Children under 16 free in South Stand.

Club shop:
Behind J.D. Matthewman Stand.
Opening hours: 10.00a.m. to 4.00p.m. Monday to Friday. Match days: from 1.30p.m.
Main items of stock: Shirts, souvenirs, old programmes.

Supporters with disabilities:
Wheelchair access or designated area: J.D. Matthewman stand.
Other special facilities: None.
Disabled toilets: North and south stands.
Access to facilities (bars etc.): Lift in north stand.
Designated car parking at ground: Four places by J.D. Matthewman stand.

Catering:
Two vans by J.D. Matthewman and south stands.
Main items on sale: Burgers, hot dogs, chips, tea & coffee, soup.
Restaurant at ground: Yes.

Bars:
Under J.D. Matthewman stand, and under south stand. Open before match.

Facilities for activities for junior supporters: None.
Match-day creche: None. Baby changing facilities in ladies toilet in J.D. Matthewman stand.
General facilities: In north stand, Royal Suite (200 people) and Ledgard Suite (75 people).
Other sports at stadium: None.
Local facilities, pubs, cafes or restaurants: The Royal Oak on Owl Lane.

Car parking:
Large car park at ground behind south stand.
Street parking: Not in immediate area - there is ample parking at the ground.

Public transport:
Information: 0113-245-7676
Nearest station: Dewsbury. From station (Huddersfield bound side): cross over ring road, go down Wellington Street and bear right at the bottom down Southgate to the bus station (¼ mile)
*Buses:*202 or 203 (Huddersfield - Leeds, half hourly) - along Leeds Road, or 205 (every 2 hours), down Owl Lane, bus stop on Windsor Road.

Directions by car:
From north, east or west: M62 junction 28. Take A653 signposted Dewsbury. Turn left into Owl Lane, left at roundabout, and ground is on right.
From south: M1 junction 40. Take A638 signposted Dewsbury. At roundabout turn right into Owl Lane (Leeds/Batley, not Dewsbury). Ground is on left.

Tourist Information:
Huddersfield Tourist Information Centre, 3-5 Albion Street, Huddersfield, W. Yorkshire, HD1 2NW.
Tel: 01484-223200 Fax: 01484-223202.

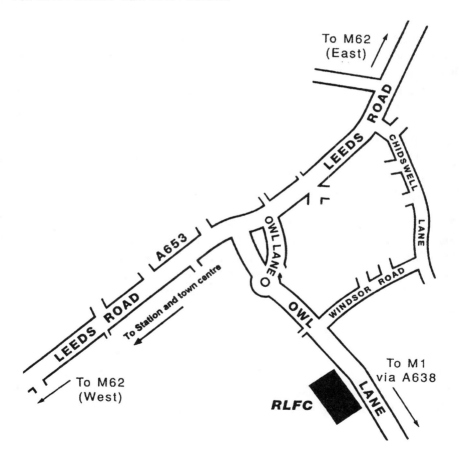

Doncaster Dragons

Ground: Belle Vue.
Address: Bawtry Road, Doncaster, DN4 5HT.
Telephone: Club moving offices - not available when book went to print.
Fax: Club moving offices - not available when book went to print.
Website: www.doncasterdragons.org.uk
E-mail: doncasterdragons@btinternet.com
Capacity: 7,200
Number of seats: 1,250

History of ground:
The Belle Vue stadium has the distinction of sharing then same name as the home of Wakefield Trinity Wildcats. The ground is the home of Doncaster Rovers FC who play in the Vauxhall Conference.

Doncaster previously played at York Road (1951 to 1953) which had a record attendance of 10,000 for a first round, second leg Challenge Cup game against Bradford Northern in 1952. Tattersfield is perhaps the spiritual home of the game in Doncaster which hosted the club from 1953 to 1995. The record attendance was 6,440 in 1994 for the visit of Leeds. After leaving Tattersfield, the club moved to the Meadow Court stadium in Stainforth before moving to Belle Vue in 1999.

Description of ground: The main stand has some modern seats, but comprises mainly wooden seating. There are covered terraces in front and open terraces at the sides. The covered terraced stand opposite provides an unobstructed view of the pitch. The open terraces behind the goal is closed and therefore there is no access between the two stands.

Stands and terraces:
Restrictions on use: None.
Views from different areas: Some pillars in front of seats in main stand.
Under cover: Main stand side and terracing and opposite stand.
Transfers to seats: Transfer inside ground. Enter on the stand side - it is not possible to move around the ground.

Entrance price reductions:
Children: Yes.
Senior citizens: Yes.
Students: Yes with student card
Disabled: Yes - obtain pass from club office
Family tickets or reductions: For some matches.

Club shop:
Portakabin outside main stand.
Opening hours: Matchdays.
Main items of stock: Clothing.

Supporters with disabilities:
Wheelchair access or designated area: Yes, in front of main stand.
Other special facilities: None.
Disabled toilets: Main stand.
Access to facilities (bars etc.): Yes.
Designated car parking at ground: No.

Catering:
Two kiosks(each side of the ground).
Main items on sale: Burgers, hot dogs, confectionery, hot/cold drinks.
Restaurant at ground: No.

Bars:
Executive Lounge and Dragon Club (members only) both at back of main stand.

Facilities for activities for junior supporters: None.
Match-day creche: None.
General facilities for hire: None.
Other sports at stadium: Football (Doncaster Rovers)
Local facilities, pubs, cafes or restaurants: Pub at nearby roundabout.

Car parking:
Plenty of parking at ground.
Street parking: None in immediate area

Public transport:
Information: 01302-344949 or 01709-515151
Nearest station: Doncaster. 2 miles from ground.

Buses: There are three bus stations in the town centre - North and South (travel to and from other towns) Duke Street (local routes). From train station and North bus station : cross Trafford Way via subway. Walk through Frenchgate shopping mall to exit onto Sepulchre Gate. Turn right, then first left into Duke Street bus station. Catch number 170 (every 15 minutes) or 58A (every 20 minutes) Bus stop is opposite ground on Bawtry Road, on Carr House Road for return journey.

Directions by car:
From east or west: at J33 of M62. turn south along A1-A1(M). At J36 turn east along A630 Warmsworth Road - Balby Road. Bear right into A18, Carr House Road and at roundabout turn right into Bawtry Road. Ground and car park on right.
From north or south: A1 - A1(M) to J36, then as above.

Tourist Information:
Doncaster Tourist Information Centre, Central Library, Waterdale, Doncaster, S. Yorkshire DN1 3JE.
Tel.: 01302-734309. Fax: 01302-735385.

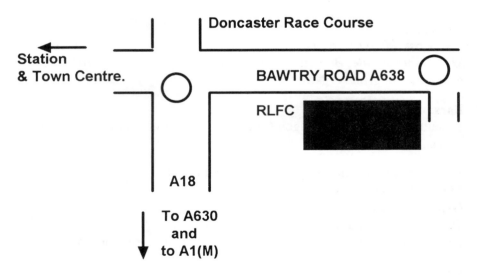

Featherstone Rovers

Ground: Lionheart Stadium.
Address: Lionheart Stadium, Post Office Road, Featherstone WF7 5EN.
Telephone: 01977-702386.
Fax: 01977-602675
Website: www.btinternet.com/~rovers/fev.html
E-mail: None
Capacity: 7,000 (approx.)
Number of seats: 2,500 (approx.)

History of ground: Post Office Road, now known as the Lionheart Stadium is one of the most evocative of all Rugby League grounds. It is closely linked with the local working class mining community and a pit was once clearly visible from one end of the ground. The old main stand was inaugurated during the 1926 miners strike, the club being formed at the same public house which staged the enquiry into the massacre of local miners in 1893 at a nearby colliery. Rovers previously played at the Featherstone Main Colliery Welfare ground in 1912-13. The first game at Post Office Road was played in 1921 in front of 4,000 fans, the record attendance being 17,531 for a Challenge Cup third round game against St Helens in 1959, the crowd being somewhat bigger than the size of Featherstone's population. The original floodlights were inaugurated in 1983, and the new Main Stand was built in 1991. Since then, the new covered seated RJB Family Stand has been completed.

Featherstone got a great deal of publicity in the 1995 campaign against club mergers, when proposals to merge them with local rivals Castleford and Wakefield would have destroyed one of the game's great traditional small town clubs.

Description of ground: Two modern cantilever stands on the sides of the pitch, with open terracing behind both goals. Enough seats for the club to play at a higher level.

Stands and terraces:
Restrictions on use: None.
Views from different areas: No obstructions in either stand.
Under cover: Both stands.

25

Transfers to seats: Payment in ground to transfer to Main Stand. No charge for sitting in the RJB Family Stand.

Entrance price reductions:

Children: Yes.

Senior citizens: Yes.

Students: No.

Disabled: No.

Family tickets or reductions: Family tickets available.

Club shop:
By Main Stand. Supporters club shop near turnstiles by car park.
Opening hours: Club shop: Monday & Friday: 9.00a.m. to 4.00p.m. Tuesday, Wednesday & Thursday: 9.00a.m. to 4.30p.m. Saturday: 9.15a.m. to 11.00a.m. Sunday match days: 1 hour before kick off. Supporters club shop: Open on match days.
Main items of stock: Club shop: Shirts, videos and souvenirs. Details on club website. Supporters club: Badges and old programmes.

Supporters with disabilities:
Wheelchair access or designated area: Front of Main Stand.
Other special facilities: None.
Disabled toilets: Two behind Family Stand.
Access to facilities (bars etc.): No.
Designated car parking at ground: Back of Main stand.

Catering:
Two burger bars behind Main stand. Tea bar behind goal.
Main items on sale: Burger bars: Burgers, hot dogs, tea & coffee etc. Tea bar: Tea & coffee, pies, Bovril and soup.
Restaurant at ground: No.

Bars:
Upstairs behind Main stand.

Facilities for activities for junior supporters: None.
Match-day creche: None.
General facilities for hire: Function rooms for hire in Main stand.
Other sports at stadium: None.
Local facilities, pubs, cafes or restaurants: The Railway across the road from the ground. Other local pubs.

Car parking:
Adequate parking at ground for most matches.
Street parking: Some in side streets.

Public transport:
Information:
0113-245-7676
Nearest station:
Featherstone station 100 yards from ground. One train per hour, none on Sundays.
Buses: 143, 144, 146, 177, 183 (Castleford / Pontefract). 177 & 183 only on Sundays. 180 & 181 to Normanton. Sunday afternoon one every 2 hours.

Directions by car:
M62 take junction 32, A639 to Pontefract. Pass race course, and turn right onto B6134. Turn left onto B6421, follow road towards town centre, cross railway, and Post Office Road is on right.

Coming from Wakefield, take A645, and turn left onto B6421. Ground is then on right just before railway and station.

Tourist Information:
Wakefield Tourist Information, Town Hall, Wood Street, Wakefield, W. Yorkshire, WF1 2HQ.
Tel.: 01924-305000. Fax: 01924-305775

Gateshead Thunder

Ground: Gateshead International Stadium
Address: Gateshead International Stadium, Neilson Road, Gateshead, Tyne & Wear, NE10 0EF.
Telephone: 0191-4400161
Fax: 0191-4400163
Website: www.gateshead-thunder.com
E-mail: thunder1@easynet.co.uk
Capacity: 11,795
Number of seats: 11,795

History of ground: The stadium was built in the 1960s, primarily as an athletics venue. Since 1977, it has been the home of Gateshead FC. This is a different club from the one that played in the Football league until 1960. A former ground of their's was Horsley Hill, where the South Shields Rugby League team played from 1901 to 1904. Professional club Rugby League was played in Newcastle for a couple of seasons in the 1930s, but then did not return until Gateshead Thunder joined Super League in 1999. This was after along period of development in the north east, including an academy team based in Gateshead and international matches being staged at the International Stadium. But a successful first season on the pitch, matched with encouraging attendances, ended in heartbreak for the club's supporters when the club "merged" with Hull.

But a local group of supporters kept the Thunder name alive, and the club entered the Northern Ford Premiership for the 2000-2001 season, again using the International Stadium as a base.

Description of ground: An athletics stadium that may prove too big for the crowds for Northern Ford Premiership games. It offers good facilities, but as with Sheffield, and Crystal Palace in the past, may lack atmosphere. It may also be rather bleak in winter.

Stands and terraces:
Restrictions on use: Only one stand is used. No restrictions.
Views from different areas: Clear, no obstructions.
Under cover: Main stand.
Transfers to seats: Not applicable.

Entrance price reductions:
Children: Yes.   *Disabled:* Yes
Senior citizens: Yes.   *Family tickets or reductions:* Yes -
Students: Yes.   must be pre booked.

Club shop:
At stadium.
Opening hours: Match days 2.00 p.m. to 5.00 p.m. Weekdays 9.00a.m. to 5.00 p.m.
Main items of stock: Full range of clothing and other merchandise

Supporters with disabilities:
Wheelchair access or designated area: At front of stand
Other special facilities: None
Disabled toilets: Main stand
Access to facilities (bars etc.): Yes.
Designated car parking at ground: Contact club for details.

Catering:
Under main stand.
Main items on sale: Pies, pasties, burgers, tea & coffee, cold drinks.
Restaurant at ground: No.

Bars:
Bar in the main stand

Facilities for activities for junior supporters:
Match-day creche: None.
General facilities for hire: Contact stadium for details.
Other sports at stadium: Athletics, football.
Local facilities, pubs, cafes or restaurants: Schooner Inn on South Shore Road. Families welcome.

Car parking:
Plenty of parking in car parks close to ground
Street parking: Limited, but should not be needed.

Public transport:
Information: 0845-6060260
Nearest station: Gateshead Stadium Metro. *Mainline:* Newcastle Central.

Buses: 93. No direct buses from Newcastle City Centre, use metro service.

Directions by car:
From south: A1/A1(M) towards Newcastle. After Washington Services, take A194(M). Turn left onto A184, towards centre of Gateshead. Turn right into Neilson Road and stadium is on right.
From Carlisle: A69 towards Newcastle, then take A1 south, and turn onto A184. Stay on A184, and turn left into Neilson Road.

Tourist Information:
Gateshead Tourist Information Centre, Metrocentre, Portcullis, 7, The Arcade, Gateshead, Tyne and Wear, NE11 9YL.
Tel: 0191-460-6345. Fax: 0191-460-4285.
Email: tic@portcullis.demon.co.uk

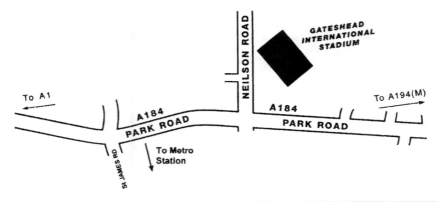

Gateshead versus Hull Kingston Rovers, the club's first match in the Northern Ford Premiership, 3 December 2000. Photo: Mike Haddon

Halifax Blue Sox

Ground: Shay Stadium
Address: The New Pavilion, Shay Stadium, Halifax HX1 2YS.
Telephone: 01422-342792. Club shop: 01422-300104.
Fax: 01422-349607. Club shop: 01422-300106.
Website: www.bluesox.co.uk
E-mail: murgatroyd@breathe.co.uk
Capacity: 13,000 (when redevelopment complete).
Number of seats: Not known - redevelopment not completed.

History of ground:
The Shay is shared with Third Division football neighbours Halifax Town FC and has been substantially improved since the Blue Sox moved in. Halifax Town have played at The Shay since 1921, when the club joined the Football League. The ground has also staged speedway in the past.

However, most rugby league people who think of Halifax can't help but remember their original ground, the marvellously named Thrum Hall. This was their home from 1886 until 1998, and hosted a record attendance of 29,153 for the visit of Wigan for a third round Challenge Cup tie in 1959. The atmospheric if somewhat Victorian ground had 1,218 seats in a capacity of less than 10,000 in its later years and like neighbours Huddersfield and Leeds backed onto a cricket ground. The ground hosted the Challenge Cup final in 1914 and Championship finals in 1912, 1929 and 1930.

Description of ground: The redevelopment of the ground makes it almost unrecognisable from a decade ago. The Skircoat Stand has both standing and seating areas. There is covered terracing behind both goals, with the South Terrace being under cover. The East Stand was being built at the time of writing, but when completed will provide further seating areas. When the work is finished, it will be an excellent venue for Super League, with adequate seating and terraced areas.

Stands and terraces:
Restrictions on use: None.
Views from different areas: Skircoat Stand has some pillars. Otherwise unobstructed.
Under cover: Both stands and South Terrace.

31

Transfers to seats: Skircoat stand has seating and terracing - no transfer charge. There are no transfers within the ground - supporters must stay in the part of the ground they enter.

Entrance price reductions:
Children: Yes (16 and under).
Senior citizens: Yes.
Students: Yes.
Disabled: Free of charge to wheelchair user and escort. Contact club for further details.
Family tickets or reductions: No.

Club shop:
The Blue Sox Connexion, 24, Union Street, Halifax HX1 1PR.
Opening hours: Office hours.
Main items of stock: Clothing, souvenirs etc.

Supporters with disabilities:
Wheelchair access or designated area: East stand and front of Hunger Hill (north) terrace.
Other special facilities: No.
Disabled toilets: Yes.
Access to facilities (bars etc.): No.
Designated car parking at ground: Limited amount at Hunger Hill terrace end.

Catering:
South Terrace: Burger van and sweet shop. Skircoat stand: Burger bar. North terrace: Burger bar.
Main items on sale: Burgers, hot dogs, soup, cold drinks, tea & coffee. Good selection of sweets at sweet shop.
Restaurant at ground: No.

Bars:
South Stand lounge - members only. No other bars for supporters at the ground.

Facilities for activities for junior supporters: None
Match-day creche: None
General facilities for hire: The Weavers - contact 01422-368818
Other sports at stadium: Football (Halifax Town FC)

Local facilities: The Shay pub at north end of ground on corner Hunger Hill and South Parade. Others in area.

Car parking:
No public parking at ground.
Street parking: Some street parking in local area. Pay car parks in town centre.

Public transport:
Information: 0113-245-7676
Nearest station: Halifax. Turn left past Eureka! (¼ mile)
Buses: Bus station is ½ mile from the ground. Exit at higher end and turn left, or at lower end and turn right.

Directions by car:
The Shay is on the A629, on the south side of Halifax.
From the west: M62, junction 24: A629 signposted Halifax. Stay on A629, then fork right, signposted The Shay, into Free School Lane, which becomes Shaw Hill. Ground is on left. Ground is well signposted in town.
From the east: M62, junction 26: Follow A58 into Halifax. Follow signs for Eureka! and the railway station (some signs include The Shay) and the ground is 200 yards past Eureka!

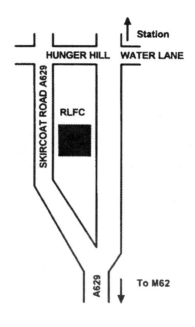

Tourist Information:
Halifax Tourist Information Office, Piece Hall, Halifax, W. Yorkshire, HX1 1RE.
Tel: 01422-368725. Fax: 01422-354264.

33

Huddersfield Giants

Ground: Alfred McAlpine Stadium
Address: Alfred McAlpine Stadium, Leeds Road, Huddersfield,
W. Yorkshire HD1 6PZ.
Tel: 01484-530710
Fax: 01484-531712
Website: www.giantsonline.co.uk Stadium: www.mcalpinestadium.com
E-mail: enquiries@giantsonline.co.uk
Capacity: 24,500
Seats: 24,500

History of ground: The Alfred McAlpine Stadium (the Big Mac to its fans) is now the home of the Giants (Fartown to the traditionalists). The ultra-modern all-seater stadium was opened in 1995, with the final stand being completed in 1998. The ground has become a regular venue for important Rugby League matches, including World Cup semi-finals in 1995 and 2000, both classic matches, and Challenge Cup semi-finals.

The club's original ground, Fartown, will always be a part of Rugby League history. The first game was in 1878 and had a record attendance of 35,136 for a Challenge Cup semi-final in 1947. The ground had a large terrace along one side of the ground and had floodlights installed in 1967. The ground was home to a soccer FA Cup semi-final and hosted the Challenge Cup finals in 1908 and 1911 plus Championship Finals in 1907 and 1936 and the 1979 Premiership Final.

The new ground seems to have become a successful ground-share between Rugby League and football, with the local council also involved.

Description of ground: Architecturally impressive modern all-seater stadium, shared with Huddersfield Town F.C. Unobstructed view from all sections but only the Lawrence Batley and John Smith stands utilised for most Super League matches.

Stands and terraces:
Restrictions on use: None.
Views from different areas: All unobstructed.
Under cover: All stands.

Transfers to seats: Not applicable. No transfers within ground.

Entrance price reductions:
Children: Yes.
Senior citizens: Yes.
Students: Yes – college card needed.

Disabled: Yes
Family tickets or reductions: Contact club for details.

Club shop:
Stadium superstore between Lawrence Batley and main car park.
Opening hours: Two hours before the match and ½ hour afterwards. Also normal office hours.
Main items of stock: Some general leisure-wear stocked in addition to Giants and Huddersfield Town F.C. shirts, kit and other souvenirs.

Supporters with disabilities:
Wheelchair access or designated area: Yes. Contact club for details.
Other special facilities: Earphones for the blind in reserved seats.
Disabled toilets: Yes.
Access to facilities: Ramp into club shop, automatic door into health and leisure club, staffed gates into stadium near main turnstiles.
Designated car parking at ground: Contact club for details.

Catering
Health & leisure club (in Lawrence Batley stand), Foster's Café Bar, food kiosks inside stadium
Main items on sale: Tea, coffee, soup, popcorn, light meals, pies.
Restaurant at ground: Special lunch on match days. Contact club for details.

Bars:
Foster's Café Bar. Bar in health club is members only.

Facilities for activities for junior supporters: Some pre-match entertainment.
Match-day creche: None.
General facilities: Function rooms available for hire. Contact club for details.
Other sports at stadium: Football (Huddersfield Town F.C.).

Local facilities: The George Hotel, St. George's Square – the birthplace of Rugby League. In the town centre. A nice place for a pre-match drink, and see the plaque marking the founding of the game and the display on the game's history.

Car parking:
Adequate car parking at ground for most matches, but can be slow to clear after game.
Street parking: None close to the ground. Parking in town centre can be used to avoid congestion.

Public transport:
Information: 0113-245-7676
Nearest station: Huddersfield. ¾ mile from ground. Good café bar there. Left out of station, pass George Hotel, into Northumberland Street. At end of street, go straight across into Leeds Road (A62). At roundabout, go right into Gas Works Street. This leads to Stadium Way.
Buses: Bus station one mile from ground. Follow signs for A62 - Leeds Road, then as from station. Buses to Leeds or along Leeds Road, including 201,202,203,217,218,219,220,221 and 229.

Directions by car:
From west: M62 take junction 25, take A644 towards Dewsbury, and turn right onto A62. Stay on A62 into Huddersfield, and stadium is on left.
From east: M62 take junction 24, A629 to Huddersfield. Turn left on ring road, and then left onto A62. Stadium is on right.
From south: M1 take junction 38, A637 to Huddersfield. Left onto A642, turn right on ring road, and right onto A62. Stadium on right.

Tourist Information:
Huddersfield Tourist Information, 3-5 Albion Street, Huddersfield, W. Yorkshire, HD1 2NW.
Tel: 01484-223200. Fax: 01484-223202.

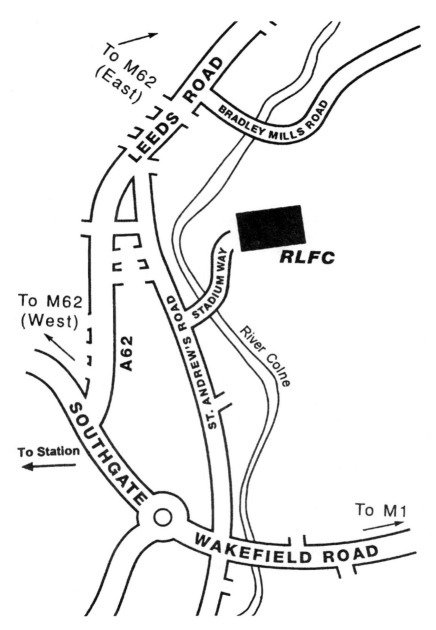

Hull F.C.

Ground: The Boulevard Ground.
Address: The Boulevard Ground, Airlie Street, Hull, HU3 3JD.
Telephone: 01482-327200
Fax: 01482-587002
Website: www.hullfc.com
E-mail: hullfc@stadium.freeserve.co.uk
Capacity: 12,000
Number of seats: 2,500

History of ground: The Boulevard has nostalgic connotations for many Rugby League fans. With its Threepenny stand and raucous atmosphere it is a typical traditional League ground. Its history goes back to 1895 when Liversedge were the visitors for the first match, with an 8,000 crowd. Its record attendance was 28,798 for the visit of Leeds for a Challenge Cup third round game in 1936. New floodlights were installed in 1990. Four Great Britain Tests have been played at the ground and it has also been used for matches in the 1970, 1995 and 2000 World Cups. Other grounds used by Hull FC have been the Hull City FC ground at Boothferry Park for joint tourist games with Hull KR, and various grounds from 1865 to 1895.

Description of ground: The East Stand and the Roy Waudby Threepenny Stand provide seating, with the latter also having a standing area. But behind both goals is open terracing, not very near the pitch because of the old speedway track. Plans to move to a new all-seater stadium are now in place, with The Boulevard remaining as a training venue and community development centre. Following crowd problems involving some Hull fans at the 2000 Challenge Cup semi-final, the club have put considerable efforts into making The Boulevard more welcoming for away supporters. An away supporters liaison officer now welcomes all away coaches and fans.

Stands and terraces:
Restrictions on use: None. Junior enclosure in East Stand.
Views from different areas: Threepenny stand and behind goals - no obstructions. Some pillars in East Stand.
Under cover: Both stands. Open behind goals.
Transfers to seats: Upgrade to East Stand only inside ground.

Entrance price reductions:
Children: Yes
Senior citizens: Yes
Students: No
Disabled: Yes - wheelchair bound

only.
Family tickets or reductions:
Contact club for details.

Club shop:
By Airlie Street entrance (outside ground) and by East Stand at Airlie Street end. Also at the Top Deck, Princes Quay shopping centre.
Opening hours: Office hours and match days.
Main items of stock: Good choice of shirts, clothing and souvenirs.

Supporters with disabilities:
Wheelchair access or designated area: Front of Roy Waudby Threepenny Stand.
Other special facilities: None.
Disabled toilets: Behind East Stand at Airlie Street end.
Access to facilities (bars etc.): To bar in Roy Waudby Threepenny Stand.
Designated car parking at ground: Contact club.

Catering:
Behind East Stand and behind Roy Waudby Threepenny Stand.
Main items on sale: Burgers, tea & coffee, cold drinks, sweets, chocolate.
Restaurant at ground: No.

Bars:
Boulevard Bar in Roy Waudby Threepenny Stand. Rugby Suite on terracing at Airlie Street end. Away supporters use the Rugby Suite.

Facilities for activities for junior supporters: Pre-match entertainment - bouncy castle, face painting, etc.
Match-day creche: None.
General facilities for hire: Contact club for details.
Other sports at stadium: None.
Local facilities, pubs, cafes or restaurants: Pubs and cafes in area around ground.

Car parking:
Limited parking at ground.

Street parking: Some in nearby streets. Some restrictions.

Public transport:
Information: 01482-222222
Nearest station: Hull Paragon. Turn right onto Ferensway, then left onto Anlaby Road. In approximately ½mile, turn left into Saner Street then right into Queensgate. This leads to The Boulevard and Airlie Street is opposite.
Buses: Hull Corporation 1 & 2 from Central Bus station. 9F from Hull Station.
EYMS: 60,64,66,151,155,181 from Central Bus station.

Directions by car:
M62 to Hull, then A63 into city. Pass cinema & ten pin bowling on right, and take next exit. At roundabout, turn left into Hessle Road, and right into Boulevard. Ground is on left, off Airlie Street.

Tourist Information:
1, Paragon Street, Hull, East Yorkshire, HU1 3NA.
Tel: 01482-223559. Fax: 01482-613959.

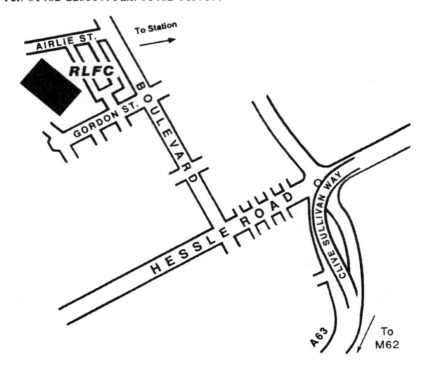

Hull Kingston Rovers

Ground: Craven Park..
Address: Craven Park, Preston Road, Hull HU9 5HE.
Telephone: 01482-374648 Lotteries: 01482-702726
Fax: 01482-791586
Website: www.hullkr.co.uk
E-mail: webmaster@hullkr.co.uk
Capacity: 8,500
Number of seats: 1,992

History of ground: Craven Park, Hull is one of the most famous names of all Rugby League grounds. The original ground was Rovers' home from 1922-1989, the (new) Craven Park became the club's home in September 1989. The record attendance at Preston Road is 8,500 for the visit of Hull FC in 1990. The old Craven Park had a record attendance of 22,282 for a league game versus Hull in 1922. Hull KR had a record attendance of 27,670 for a league game against Hull in 1953 at Boothferry Park. Hull KR have also played at various local grounds prior to 1922 including Craven Street and Holderness Road which had a record crowd of 18,000 in 1914.

Description of ground: The ground has a large main stand, the West Stand, which provides an excellent view from the seats. The main covered terracing area is the East Stand. There are also small terracing areas in front of the West Stand and at the scoreboard (south) end. The two stands are impressive, however, the south end of the ground faces the sea, making it very cold. The West Stand includes a function room, executive boxes and the club's offices and shop. The ground could host Super League matches, but needs development at the scoreboard end to give it more atmosphere and reduce the cold winds. The pitch is also often very muddy in winter, producing low scoring games with players covered in mud - a reminder of past times in the game.

Stands and terraces:
Restrictions on use: None.
Views from different areas: Pillars in both stands, but good views.
Under cover: Both stands.
Transfers to seats: Pay at turnstiles.

Entrance price reductions:

Children: Yes.

Senior citizens: Yes.

Students: No.

Disabled: No.

Family tickets or reductions: No.

Club shop:

Outside ground in West Stand.

Opening hours: Monday to Friday 9a.m. to 4.30p.m. Saturday: 9a.m. to 12 noon, and two hours before kick-off on match days.

Main items of stock: Shirts, good selection of souvenirs.

Supporters with disabilities:

Wheelchair access or designated area: On track by West Stand.

Other special facilities: None.

Disabled toilets: Under West Stand.

Access to facilities (bars etc.): No.

Designated car parking at ground: Five places by entrance to main stand.

Catering:

Burger van by West Stand and behind East Stand.

Main items on sale: Burgers, hot dogs, sweets, crisps, tea & coffee.

Restaurant at ground: Yes - pre-match meals in West Stand.

Bars:

West stand - members only.

Facilities for activities for junior supporters: None.

Match-day creche: None.

General facilities for hire: Function rooms for hire in West Stand.

Other sports at stadium: Greyhound racing and speedway.

Local facilities, pubs, cafes or restaurants: The Crown pub on corner of Preston Road and Marfleet Lane.

Car parking:

Plenty of parking at ground.

Street parking: Restricted near the ground in Preston Road.

Public transport:

Information: 01482-222222.

Nearest station: Hull Paragon. Over 3 miles from the ground.

Buses: Buscall, EYMS and Stagecoach. 41, 42 from bus station (hourly on Sundays).

Directions by car: Craven Park is in east Hull. M62, then A63 into city. Stay on A63, and at roundabout turn right into A1033, Hedon Road. Turn left into Marfleet Avenue, and fork left into Marfleet Lane. Turn right into Preston Road, and ground is on right behind supermarket. The ground is signposted.

Tourist Information:
1, Paragon Street, Hull, East Yorkshire, HU1 3NA.
Telephone: 01482-223559. Fax: 01482-613959.

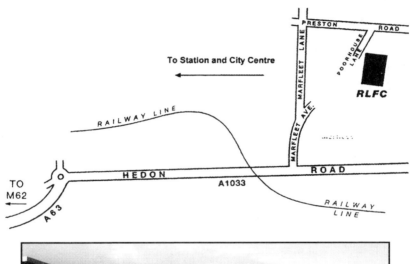

Craven Park: Hull KR versus Sheffield Eagles January 2000

Hunslet Hawks

Ground: South Leeds Stadium.
Address: South Leeds Stadium, Middleton Grove, Leeds LS11 5DJ.
Telephone: 0113-271-1675   Commercial: 0113-271-2730
Fax: 0113-270-1198
Clubcall: 09068-121130
Website: None
E-mail: jdracup@freeserve.co.uk
Capacity: 2,471
Number of seats: 2,471

History of ground: The South Leeds Stadium has been Hunslet's home since 1995, following a nomadic period since leaving Parkside in 1973, and reforming as a new club. Parkside was the home of the club for 85 years from 1888 to1973 and had a record attendance of 24,700 for a third round Challenge Cup game in 1924. Hunslet originally played at Woodhouse Hill, from 1883 to 1888, and after leaving Parkside played at Elland Road Greyhound Stadium from 1973 to 1979. That ground had the distinction of using a helicopter to dry the pitch for a Challenge Cup game against Warrington in 1975, and having American Football style goalposts. The club has also been based at Leeds United's Elland Road ground, with crowds of a few hundred in a huge stadium; Batley's Mount Pleasant and Bramley's McLaren Field. Now the club is back in their traditional south Leeds base, near to their original much-loved Parkside home.

Description of ground: The pitch is surrounded by an athletics track, with one very modern cantilever stand. This is adequate for most of Hunslet's matches, but the grass banks around the pitch have been used for important matches in the end of season play-offs. To progress further, more development of the ground is necessary, as the club found when they tried to join Super League.

Stands and terraces:
Restrictions on use: None.
Views from different areas: All clear and unobstructed.
Under cover: Yes, but the stand has no sides, so the rain can blow in.
Transfers to seats: Not applicable.

44

Entrance price reductions:

Children: Yes.

Senior citizens: Yes.

Students: No.

Disabled: No.

Family tickets or reductions: No.

Club shop:

Behind reception in main entrance.

Opening hours: Match days. Contact club office otherwise.

Main items of stock: Good selection of souvenirs, shirts, clothing.

Supporters with disabilities:

Wheelchair access or designated area: In main stand.

Other special facilities: Lift by reception.

Disabled toilets: Ground floor near reception. Top tier of stand.

Access to facilities (bars etc.): On ground floor.

Designated car parking at ground: Yes.

Catering:

Two bars and tea bar on top tier of stand.

Main items on sale: Bar on ground floor has drinks and a few snacks. Other bar also has burgers, hot dogs, sweets, chocolate etc. Tea bar has tea & coffee, pies and chocolate.

Restaurant at ground: No.

Bars:

Two in main stand.

Facilities for activities for junior supporters: None.

Match-day creche: None.

General facilities: Phoenix bar, holds up to 50 people, for conferences and seminars.

Other sports at stadium: Athletics, tennis centre, five-a-side football.

Local facilities, pubs, cafes or restaurants: No pubs near stadium.

Car parking:
Plenty of parking at ground.
Street parking:
None on Middleton Grove, some off Dewsbury Road.

Public transport:
Information: 0113-245-7676.
Nearest station: Leeds City. 2½ miles from ground.
Buses: None run to Stadium, stop on Dewsbury Road.
Sundays: 117, 201, 202, 203, 280, 281. Not on Sundays: 116, 118, 216, 218, 220, 226, 227, X7.

Directions by car:
M621 junction 5 for Hunslet & Beeston. From south, turn left on Tunstall Road. Turn left and Middleton Grove is half a mile on the left. There is no exit from junction 5 if coming from the north. Take A653 from city centre. The stadium is well signposted.

To station and city centre

A653

TUNSTALL ROAD

Junction 5

M621

DEWSBURY ROAD

M1 south and M62 (east)

A653

MIDDLETON GROVE

RLFC

M62 (west)

Tourist Information:
Gateway Yorkshire, PO Box 244, The Arcade, City Station, Leeds, W. Yorkshire LS1 1PL.
Tel: 0113-242-5242. Fax: 0113-246-8246.

Keighley Cougars

Ground: Cougar Park.
Address: Cougar Park, Royd Ings Avenue, Keighley, BD21 3RF.
Telephone: 01535-213111
Fax: 01535-213100
Website: www.cougars.co.uk
E-mail: gary@cougars.fsnet.co.uk
Capacity: 5,500
Number of seats: 1,200

History of ground: Cougar Park, formerly known as Lawkholme Lane, is one of the games more rural and attractive settings, being surrounded by Ilkley Moor. It has been the home of Keighley since 1895 and the record attendance was14,500 for the visit of Halifax in 1951 for a Challenge Cup third round game. Floodlights were installed in 1967 and opened by a visit from Wakefield Trinity. Television first made its appearance at the ground for the visit of the touring Australians in 1952. The club staged its first international in 1995, when Fiji played South Africa in the World Cup. Keighley previously played at Holmes' Field 1876-1878 and Dalton Lane 1878-1885.

Description of ground: The stand on the west side of the ground provides seating under cover. There is covered terracing behind one goal and open terracing elsewhere. The ground has Cougar logos and other material well displayed and has a good atmosphere. It is fine for the club's Northern Ford Premiership matches, but will need further development if the club achieves its Super League aspirations.

Stands and terraces:
Restrictions on use: None.
Views from different areas: Pillars in the seating and covered areas, but generally good views.
Under cover: Main stand and behind one goal.
Transfers to seats: Pay inside ground.

Entrance price reductions:
Children: Yes.   *Senior citizens:* Yes.

Students: Under passports to leisure scheme.
leisure scheme.
Disabled: Under passports to

Family tickets or reductions: No.

Club shop: In Keighley Town Centre, Cavendish Court
Matchdays : behind main stand. Also supporters club shop.
Opening hours: Contact club for details. Supporters club shop: match days.
Main items of stock: Contact club for details. Supporters club shop: Old programmes, souvenirs, badges, sweets.

Supporters with disabilities:
Wheelchair access or designated area: Area in front of stand.
Other special facilities: None.
Disabled toilets: Behind main stand.
Access to facilities (bars etc.): Bar under main stand.
Designated car parking at ground: Supporters Club car park 200 yards down road in Royd Ing Ave.

Catering:
Burger bar at open end by turnstiles, and behind main stand at covered end.
Main items on sale: Burgers, hot dogs, chips, curry and chips, tea & coffee.
Restaurant at ground: Yes.

Bars:
Under main stand. Includes Keighley Hall of Fame photos and display.

Facilities for activities for junior supporters: Freddie Club Under 12 (1-1½ hours before kick-off)
Match-day creche: None.
General facilities: Suites for hire for functions.
Other sports at stadium: None.
Local facilities, pubs, cafes or restaurants: No pubs in immediate vicinity of ground.

Car parking:
No parking at ground.
Street parking: Limited near ground. Parking in leisure centre.

Public transport:
Information: 0113-245-7676.
Nearest station: Keighley. Leave station onto Bradford Road. Turn right. At roundabout with Hard Ings Road turn left and ground is on right.
Buses: Keighley Bus station on Lawkholme Lane, about ¼ mile from the ground..
Bus: 78. Keighley & District travel: 01535-603284.

Directions by car:
From west: M62 take junction 24, A629 signposted Halifax. Stay on A629 to Keighley. Turn right at roundabout, and straight over second roundabout, to join A650 in Keighley. Ground is on A650 on the left. Main entrance on Royd Ings Avenue, on right off A650.
From east: M62 take junction 26, M606 to Bradford. Take A6177 (fifth exit), and turn left onto A650. Stay on A650, then as above.

Tourist Information:
Haworth Tourist Information Centre, 2-4 West Lane, Haworth, W. Yorkshire, BD22 8EF. Tel.: 01535-642329. Fax: 01535-647721.

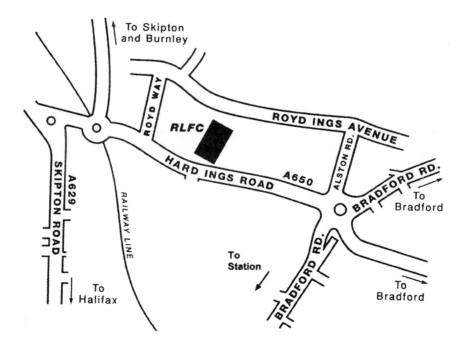

49

Leeds Rhinos

Ground: Headingley.
Address: St. Michael's Lane, Headingley, Leeds,
West Yorkshire, LS6 3BR.
Tel: 0113 278 6181
Fax: 0113 230 7617
Website: www.leedsrugby.com
E-mail: info@leedsrugby.com
Capacity: 25,000
Seats: 5,713

History of ground: Headingley is one of the most famous sports venues in the world. The ground opened in 1890. Leeds previously played at the Militia Barracks, from 1870 to 1888 and Cardigan Field from 1889 to 1890. It is unique in Rugby League grounds as the main stand has two sides and is shared with Yorkshire CCC. The cricket ground is a current Test match venue. The record attendance of 40,175 was set in 1947 for the visit of Bradford Northern in a league game .

Apart from the new joint stand, the ground has not substantially altered since the 1930s with the main addition being floodlights which were installed in 1966, and then modernised in 1988 and first used for the visit of Wakefield Trinity in a Yorkshire Cup second round game. Another innovation was the first electronic scoreboard at a Rugby League ground in 1981 at the Kirkstall Lane end. The ground has seen twelve Challenge Cup finals, eleven Championship and Premiership finals, over thirty Test matches, World Cup games, as well as Challenge Cup semi-finals and other major matches.

Description of ground: Headingley is undisputedly one of the sport's great venues, but is now showing its age and is in urgent need of modernisation. Parts of the main stand do not offer good views, and both the terraces behind the goal are open to the elements. The south stand has a great atmosphere, but is a large terrace characteristic of another age. The problem the club faces is how to redevelop the ground within a relatively confined space, and link with modernisation of the cricket ground, which faces similar problems.

Stands and terraces:
Restrictions on use: None.
Views from different areas: Some obstructions in seats and south stand.
Under cover: Main stand and south stand.
Transfers to seats: Inside ground, buy tickets by bar on cricket ground side of main stand.

Entrance price reductions:

Children: Yes.   *Disabled:* No.
Senior citizens: Yes.   *Family tickets or reductions:* No.
Students: Yes.

Ticket office is on St Michael's Lane, next to club shop. Open 9.00a.m. to 5.00p.m. Monday to Friday, 9.00a.m. to 12.30p.m. Saturday. Or telephone: 0113-278-6181 ext.229.

Club shop:
Near ground entrance in St. Michael's Lane.
Opening hours: Office hours and match days.
Main items of stock: A good selection of shirts, badges, souvenirs, mugs and flags.

Supporters with disabilities:
Wheelchair access or designated area: Front of South Stand.
Other special facilities: Commentary for blind supporters. Contact club.
Disabled toilets: By sports bar on cricket ground side of main stand.
Access to facilities: Yes to some bars.
Designated car parking at ground: Yes. Contact club for details.

Catering:
Bars, burger bars and coffee stalls in stands around ground, including on cricket ground side at scoreboard end.
Main items on sale: Burgers, chips, tea and coffee.
Restaurant at ground: Yes.

Bars:
Main stand and around ground.

Facilities for activities for junior supporters: None.
Match-day creche: No.

General facilities for hire: Suites available - contact club for details.
Other sports at stadium: Rugby union, cricket (next door).
Local facilities, pubs, cafes or restaurants: Some pubs near ground. Chip shop across road at Kirkstall Lane exit from cricket ground.

Car parking:
No car parks at ground for general public.
Street parking: restricted near ground.

Public transport:
Information: 0113-245-7676.
Nearest station: Headingley (local trains once an hour in the evenings), from Leeds City station (mainline services). From Headingley station, ¼ mile walk through to Kirkstall Lane, turn left, and enter through cricket ground on right.
Buses: 56 and 57 from station. 74, 76 and 77 from Infirmary Street.

Directions by car:
From south, east: M621 junction 2, A643 towards city centre. Join A58, then left onto A65, Kirkstall Road. After around 2 miles, turn right at traffic lights into Kirkstall Lane. Some parking in side streets, cricket ground on right. For entrance to rugby ground, turn right into Cardigan Road, and right into St Michael's Lane.
From west: M62 junction 27 take M621 to junction 2, then as above.

Tourist information:
Gateway Yorkshire, Station Arcade, PO Box 244, LS1 1PL.
Tel: 0113-242-5242.
Fax: 0113-246-8246.

To Headingley Station
and A65 (City Centre)

ST. MICHAEL'S ROAD

KIRKSTALL LANE NORTH

CARDIGAN ROAD

OTLEY ROAD

A660

HEADINGLEY LANE

A660

To City Centre
(M1,M621)

RLFC

ST. MICHAEL'S LANE

Leigh Centurions

Ground: Hilton Park
Address: Hilton Park, Kirkhall Lane, Leigh, Lancashire WN7 1RN
Telephone: 01942-743743
Fax: 01942-261843
Website: www.leigh-rugbyleague.freeserve.co.uk
E-mail: info@leigh-rugbyleague.freeserve.co.uk
Capacity: 8,000
Number of seats: 2,000

History of ground: Hilton Park is an archetypal Rugby League ground, though it is surprising to most that it was only opened in 1947. The large mill at one end of the ground summed up what some people expect to find on a northern Rugby League ground. The ground record is 31,326 for the visit of St Helens in 1953 for a Challenge Cup third round game. Hilton Park hosted a solitary Test match in 1964. Leigh previously played at Mather Lane from 1989 to1946, which had a record attendance of 25,000 for a Challenge Cup semi-final in 1930. Leigh had also played at several minor grounds between 1878 and 1889 and had played at the Athletic ground, Holden Road from 1946 to 1947.

Description of ground: Modern seating in the main stand, although the view is still obstructed by stanchions and side panels. The Kirkhall Lane stand has both terracing and bench seats. Both ends of the ground are open terracing. It would need some development for Super League.

Stands and terraces:
Restrictions on use: None.
Views from different areas: Some obstructions in both stands.
Under cover: Both stands.
Transfers to seats: Inside ground.

Entrance price reductions:
Children: Yes.   *Disabled:* Yes
Senior citizens: Yes.   *Family tickets or reductions:* Yes
Students: Yes

Club shop:
At Chadwick Street end of the ground.
Opening hours: 9-5 weekdays. 9-Noon Saturdays.
Main items of stock: Shirts, coats etc.

Supporters with disabilities:
Wheelchair access or designated area: Wheelchair area in front of the main stand.
Other special facilities: None
Disabled toilets: Yes. Other toilets accessible.
Access to facilities (bars etc.):
Designated car parking at ground:

Catering: Hilton Suite, corporate hospitality on all home games, various sponsorship packages available.
Snack bar:
Main items on sale: Meat pies, fish, chips, peas
Restaurant at ground: Yes, on match days.

Bars:
Under Kirkhall Lane stand

Facilities for activities for junior supporters: New Youth development scheme.
Match-day creche: None.
General facilities for hire: Mick Martin bar available for weddings, seminars, birthday parties etc, Hilton Suite and John Woods Suite.
Other sports at stadium: Football (Leigh RMI F.C.)
Local facilities, pubs, cafes or restaurants: Mick Martyn and Woody's

Car parking:
Plenty of parking at ground.
Street parking: In adjacent streets.

Public transport:
Information: 0161-228-7811.
Nearest stations: Atherton and Daisy Hill. No Sunday services.
Buses: From bus station, ½ mile to the ground. Turn right by George & Dragon pub along King Street, then turn left into Prescott Street or Chadwick Street.

Directions by car:

From east: M62, junction 14, take A580 (East Lancashire Road), turn right onto A579. Follow A579, passing junctions with A572 and A578. Ground is visible on right, turn right into Kirkhall Lane. Ground is behind superstore. Turn right down side of superstore, or into Glebe Street.

From north or west: M6, junction 23, take A580 east towards Manchester. Turn left into A572, then left into A579, then as above.

Tourist Information:

Wigan Tourist Information Office, Trencherfield Mill, Wallgate, Lancashire, WN3 4EL.
Tel: 01942-825677.
Fax: 01942-825677.
Email: infounit@wiganmbl.gov.uk

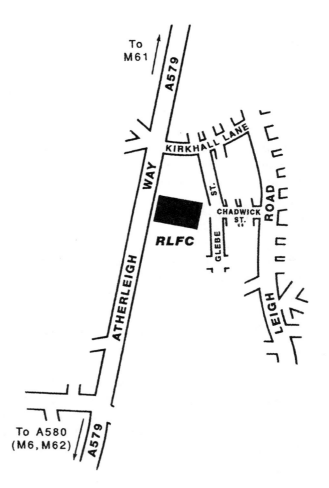

London Broncos

Ground: The Valley.
Address: The Valley, Floyd Road, Charlton, London SE7 8BL
Telephone: 020 8853 8800
Fax: 020 8853 8801
Broncoline: 09068 333 034
Website: www.londonbroncos.co.uk
E-mail: info@londonbroncos.co.uk
Capacity: 20,043
Number of seats: 20,043

History of ground: The Broncos now play at the Valley, the home of Premiership football club Charlton. The Broncos record attendance at the Valley was 10,014 for the visit of Wigan for a Super League game in 1996. The club moved back to The Valley in 2000 but had previously played there in 1995-6.

The Valley has a rich history. For many years it was an enormous football ground, with a huge terrace, which was replaced by the East Stand, its most prominent feature. In 1985, Charlton's owners suddenly moved the club to ground share with Crystal Palace. This move was hugely unpopular with supporters, culminating in a long campaign to return the club to The Valley. This included standing candidates in the local elections in 1990. The campaign was successful, with the first match "back home" in December 1992. Since then, the ground has undergone wholesale redevelopment.

For a Rugby League club with such a short history, formed as Fulham in 1980, the Londoners certainly have been around the capital. Starting off at Fulham's Craven Cottage they had a club record attendance of 15,013 for a second round Challenge Cup game against Wakefield Trinity in 1981. They have also been based at Crystal Palace National Sports Centre (1984-5 and 1990-3); Chiswick Polytechnic Sports Ground (1985-90); Barnet Copthall Stadium (1993-4) and The Stoop, Twickenham (1995-1999). Other grounds used in London are Kingsmeadow, Kingston; Claremont Road, Hendon and Griffin Park, Brentford.

Description of ground: Modernised ground with covered seating on all sides. The Broncos use the double decker West Stand but also use behind the goals for bigger games. Banks of empty seats opposite the West Stand can depress the atmosphere. Good facilities, but Rugby League still feels like tenants rather than sharers. Hopefully the club can now make the ground feel more like home. Excellent pre match activities in the car park beforehand, worth arriving early for, especially if bringing children to the game.

Stands and terraces:
Restrictions on use: Usually only main stand, other parts used for bigger games.
Views from different areas: Good.
Under cover: All areas.
Transfers to seats: Not applicable. No transfers within the ground. Supporters are expected to sit in the seat allocated to their ticket.

Entrance price reductions:
Children: Yes.   *Disabled:* Yes.
Senior citizens: Yes.   *Family tickets or reductions:* Yes.
Students: Yes.

Club shop:
On Floyd Road adjacent to ground. Also through website: www.broncoshop.co.uk
Opening hours: Normal office hours and matchdays.
Main items of stock: Shirts, books, videos, watches, stickers etc. There is a good selection of Broncos items, but, especially during the football season, Charlton items tend to dominate.

Supporters with disabilities:
Wheelchair access or designated area: Yes.
Other special facilities: None.
Disabled toilets: Yes.
Access to facilities: Yes (via lift for upstairs bars)
Designated car parking at ground: Contact club for details.

Catering:
Outside ground before game, stand concourses, and in Millennium suite (restricted access).
Main items on sale: Burgers, hot dogs, hot and cold drinks.
Restaurant at ground: Yes.

Bars:

In stand concourses, Floyds (entrance outside ground, can get very busy) and Millennium Suite - part members only.

Facilities for activities for junior supporters: Activities in the car park before the game.

Match-day creche: Yes. Family room in lower West Stand (to be confirmed - check with club).

General facilities for hire: Suites etc for hire - contact Charlton Athletic F.C. for details.

Other sports at stadium: Football (Charlton Athletic F.C.).

Local facilities: The Antigallican pub by Charlton Station. Fish and chips shop in Floyd Road.

Car parking:

Very limited parking at ground - mainly ticket holders only.

Street parking: Less limited than in 2000, when the Dome was open. Restrictions in immediate area of ground, but some street parking within 400 yards. Do not park in local trading parks - clamping operates.

Public transport:

Information: 020-7222-1234.

Nearest station: Charlton, from London Bridge, Cannon St, Waterloo East, Charing Cross and Victoria.

Nearest underground: North Greenwich underground station (Jubilee Line). Buses 486 & 472 to the ground.

Buses: 177 & 180 from Greenwich

Directions by car:

From north: Take A1, then M11. Follow signs for A406 (North Circular - **South**), stay on left, then A12 and Blackwall Tunnel. Take A12, turn right at roundabout (staying on A12), and A12 leads directly to the Blackwall Tunnel. N.B. The speed limit on the A12 changes between 40 m.p.h. and 50 m.p.h. regularly, with lots of cameras. Go through Blackwall Tunnel in left hand lane and once through tunnel, take second exit A2203. Charlton Athletic FC is well signposted from here. To get to ground, turn left at traffic lights into Woolwich Road, go right round next roundabout back onto A206 going west, and take left turning at traffic lights into Charlton Church Lane. Turn left into Floyd Road and right for club.

From other areas: A206 west from junction with A102(M), or South Circular Road (A205) to Woolwich, then A206 east to Charlton.

Tourist Information:
Greenwich Tourist Information Centre, Pepys House, Old Royal Naval College, King William Walk, Greenwich, SE10 9NN.
Tel: 0870-608-2000. Fax: 020-8853-4607.
Email: tic@greenwich.gov.uk
Local hotel: The Clarendon Hotel in Blackheath offers special deals for Broncos matches. Call the hotel on 020-8318-4321 and ask for Broncos Breaks

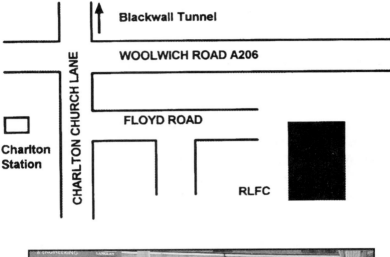

London Broncos versus Wigan at The Valley June 2000. This match marked the club's 20th anniversary and the Broncos played in the club's original kit.

Oldham Roughyeds

Ground: Boundary Park.
Address: Boundary Park, Sheepfoot Lane, Oldham, OL1 2PA
Club office: 64, Union Street, Oldham OL1 1DJ
Telephone: 0161-628-3677. Shop: 0161-627-2141.
Fax: 0161-627-5700
Website: www.oldhamroughyeds.co.uk (not working at time of writing)
E-mail: None.
Capacity: 13,500
Number of seats: 13,500

History of ground: Boundary Park is both the home of the Roughyeds and Oldham Athletic FC the town's professional soccer team. It has been Oldham Athletic's home since 1906. The Rugby League team moved in for their ill fated 1997 season in Super League. The Rugby League team then moved to play at Rochdale for a period before reaching agreement with the football club to again use Boundary Park. There is speculation about a new stadium for the two teams, but Boundary Park is adequate for both for now.

The Watersheddings was the spiritual home of the game in the town, and was the club's ground from 1889 to 1996. It had a famous slope and was one of the highest - and coldest - sporting venues in the country. The record attendance was 28,000 for the visit of Pennine neighbours Huddersfield for a league game in 1912. The ground was shared at various times with greyhounds and cricket. The ground hosted a Challenge Cup Final in 1915 and the Championship Final in 1928. The club moved to Boundary Park when the increasingly dilapidated ground was beyond repair and was sold. Oldham had previously played at Gartside Street from 1876 and then moved to Clarksfield in 1880.

Description of ground: Refurbished all seater stadium. Only some stands are opened for Rugby League matches.

Stands and terraces:
Restrictions on use: None.
Views from different areas: Unobstructed view from lower tier of George Hill stand and Rochdale Road stand.
Under cover: Yes

Transfers to seats: Not applicable. No transfers inside ground.

Entrance price reductions:

Children: Yes.

Senior citizens: Yes.

Students: No.

Disabled: No.

Family tickets or reductions: No.

Club shop:
Furtherwood Road side of ground.
Opening hours: Match days.
Main items of stock: Replica shirts, fleeces, sweatshirts, caps, flags etc.

Supporters with disabilities:
Wheelchair access or designated area: In front of Chadderton Road stand.
Other special facilities: None.
Disabled toilets: Yes.
Access to facilities (bars etc.):
Designated car parking at ground: Contact club for details.

Catering:
Kiosks in each section.
Main items on sale: Burgers, pies, hot and cold drinks, and confectionery.
Restaurant at ground: No.

Bars:
Clayton Arms on western side of ground. Small bar in George Hill stand upper tier, open at half time and after match.

Facilities for activities for junior supporters: None.
Match-day creche: No.
General facilities for hire: Contact football club for details.
Other sports at stadium: Football (Oldham Athletic F.C.)
Local facilities, pubs, cafes or restaurants: Pubs on Oldham Road.

Car parking:
Two car parks at ground. Adequate for most matches.
Street parking: Limited near to the ground.

Public transport:
*Information:*0161-228-7811

Nearest station: Oldham Werneth station, then 451 bus (hourly) to Royal Oldham Hospital. 1¼ mile walk to ground. Turn right up Featherstall Road South. Cross road before Tescos, then bear left at the roundabout along Chadderton Way as far as the Chadderton boundary sign. Turn right here into Westhulme Avenue, crossing Chadderton way via the subway.

Buses: From town centre bus stations: 412 (hourly) from Mumps (Union Street) or Town Square, or 408, 409 (3 per hour) from West Street, to the Royal Oldham Hospital.

Directions by car:
From M62, turn south at junction 20 onto A627(M). At end of motorway, take second exit along Chadderton Way (A627) and turn first left into Boundary Park Road. Or, from roundabout at end of motorway, take first exit (A663), then first right into Hilbre Avenue, which leads to car park.

Tourist Information:
Oldham Tourist Information, 11, Albion Street, Oldham, Lancs, OL1 3BD.
Tel: 0161-627-1024. Fax: 0161-911-3064.

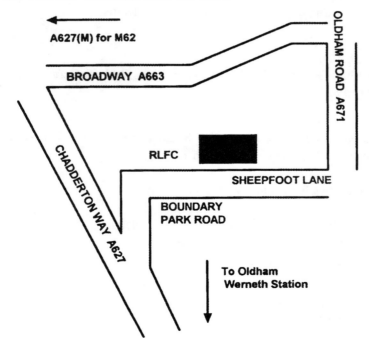

Rochdale Hornets

Ground: Spotland Stadium.
Address: Spotland Stadium, Sandy Lane, Rochdale, Lancashire, OL11 5DS.
Office address: PO Box 48, Rochdale, OL16 1PE.
Telephone: 01706-648004
Fax: None
Website: None
E-mail: None
Capacity: 10,000
Number of seats: 4,550

History of ground: Spotland is both home to Rochdale FC and the Hornets, who were founded in 1871. The record attendance for a Rugby League game is 8,150 for the visit of Oldham on Boxing Day 1989. The first Rugby League game was a one-off game in 1954 when Keighley were the visitors. Historically, the Athletic Grounds was the home of the Hornets, the club having played there from 1894 until 1988. The record attendance was 41,831 for the 1924 Challenge Cup Final. The Hornets' record crowd was 26,664 for the visit of Oldham in a third round Challenge Cup tie in 1922, the year the Hornets went on to win the Cup. Challenge Cup Finals were also staged in 1902 and 1926 and a solitary Test match in 1930. Rochdale also played at various minor grounds from 1871 until 1894. In recent times, Oldham have also played here when not based at Boundary Park.

Description of ground: Spotland is a tidy ground which has undergone considerable modernisation. The main stand and WMG stand behind the goal are modern developments, while the covered terraced areas have yet to be modernised. The WMG stand is not usually used for Rugby League matches, and there is plenty of room for the club's normal crowds.

Stands and terraces:
Restrictions on use: None.
Views from different areas: Slight obstructions by pillars, but generally good views.
Under cover: Most of the ground is under cover.
Transfers to seats: Pay at turnstiles.

63

Entrance price reductions:

Children: Yes.

Senior citizens: Yes.

Students: No.

Disabled: No.

Family tickets or reductions: No.

Club shop:

Outside ground by main entrance.

Opening hours: Match days.

Main items of stock: Shirts, souvenirs, old programmes.

Supporters with disabilities:

Wheelchair access or designated area: Wheelchair area in main stand.

Other special facilities: None.

Disabled toilets: In main stand.

Access to facilities (bars etc.): No.

Designated car parking at ground: Yes.

Catering:

Kiosks on terracing on covered side, and by turnstiles for main stand.

Main items on sale: Pies, sausage rolls, crisps, chocolate, tea & coffee.

Restaurant at ground: Yes.

Bars:

In main stand. Also sells tea & coffee.

Facilities for activities for junior supporters: None.

Match-day creche: None.

General facilities for hire: Function rooms - contact club for details.

Other sports at stadium: Football (Rochdale FC).

Local facilities, pubs, cafes or restaurants: Ratcliffe Arms by ground and Studds Supporters Bar (under WMG stand). Other pubs in area.

Car parking:

Some car parking at ground

Street parking: Some in local streets. Also at St Clements Church (junction Edenfield Road & Willbutts Lane) - donation to the church welcome.

Public transport:

Information: 0161-228-7811

Nearest station: Rochdale. 1¾ miles from ground. Taxi, or 471 bu (½ hourly) (0 to bus station. To walk to bus station (½ mile), go to end of Maclure Road & turn right onto Drake Street. Bus station is at end of Drake Street.

Buses: From bus station: 438 to After Eight Restaurant on Rooley Moor Rd at junction with Edenfield Rd; 444 to Edenfield Rd, 461 to Sandy Lane (all hourly).

Walking to the ground from station: At the end of Maclure Rd, turn left and walk to the end of Drake St. Turn right onto Manchester Rd, then left at the roundabout into Dane St, passing ASDA on the right. When Dane St forks left, keep to the main road (Mellor St), and at the end turn left into Edenfield Rd, then left again after St Clements Church into Willbutts Lane.

Directions by car:

From east or west: Take M62 to junction 20, A627(M) to Rochdale. Turn left at roundabout onto A664, and at next roundabout take second turnoff, B6452, Roch Valley Way. Stay on B6452, cross B6222 (Bury Road), B6452 now becomes Sandy Lane. Ground is on right-hand side.

Tourist Information:

Rochdale Tourist Information Centre, The Clock Tower, Town Hall, Rochdale, OL16 1AB.

Tel.: 01706-356592. Fax: 01706-864215.

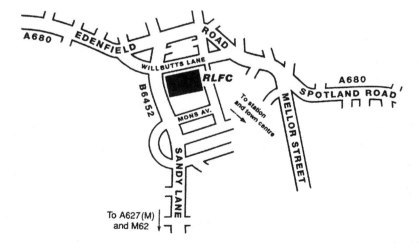

St Helens

Ground: Knowsley Road.
Address: Knowsley Road, Dunriding Lane, St Helens, WA10 4AD.
Tel: 01744-23697 (office), 01744-734103 (superstore),
01744-758269 (sales), 01744-756119 (restaurant and bars).
Fax: 01744-451302
Newsline: 09068-664422
Website: www.saints.uk.com
E-mail: info@saints.uk.com

History of ground: Knowsley Road has been the home of St Helens since 1890, and it will be a huge change when the club move to a new ground, currently planned at the end of the 2001 season. The first game was against Manchester Rangers on 6 September 1890. The record attendance was 35,695 for the visit of rivals Wigan in 1949 for a league game, the gates were however rushed and it was estimated that the attendance was in the region of 38,000. Floodlights were installed in 1965, and first used for a game against Other Nationalities which attracted 15,000 supporters. Despite the size of the ground and its imposing Kop at the Edington end of the ground the site is limited by the number of seats (2,300) and has therefore only hosted one Championship Final in 1926 and a handful of Test matches. It staged World Cup matches in 1995 and 2000.

Description of ground: Main stand and covered terracing on other side and behind one goal. It has an excellent playing surface, but the actual stadium in need of modernisation. Possibly over-used due to taking in tenants of various codes.

Stands and terraces:
Restrictions on use: None.
Views from different areas: Stand view obstructed, one corner out of sight and some obstruction from pillars. Terracing view clear.
Under cover: Partially. Clubhouse end of ground is uncovered.
Transfers to seats: Inside ground.

Entrance price reductions:
Children: Yes, up to age 16.   *Senior citizens:* Yes.

Students: Yes - NUS card needed.
Disabled: Contact club for details.

Family tickets or reductions: Family stand.

Club shop:
Outside ground at front of stadium.
Opening hours: 9.00 a.m. to 5.00 p.m. Monday to Saturday and matchdays.
Main items of stock: Replica shirts, tee-shirts, polo shirts.

Disabled supporters:
Wheelchair access or designated area: Yes.
Other special facilities: Commentaries for visually impaired.
Disabled toilets: None.
Access to facilities: Mobile catering vans, social club.
Designated car parking at ground: Contact club.

Catering:
Kiosks around ground.
Main items on sale: Burgers and hot-dogs, tea & coffee.
Restaurant at ground: Yes.

Bars:
None in ground – Saints club at scoreboard end of ground.

Facilities for activities for junior supporters: Junior St. Bernard Club
Match-day creche: None.
General facilities for hire: Social club.
Other sports at stadium: Football (Liverpool F.C reserves and St. Helens Town F.C), rugby union (Liverpool-St. Helens RUFC)
Local facilities: Black Bull pub. All local pubs can get very busy on matchdays.

Car parking:
No car parks at ground for public use.
Street parking: Many side-streets cordoned off on matchdays

Public transport:
Information: 0151-236-7676.
Nearest station: St Helens Central, 1½ miles from ground. Down Shaw Street, turn right into Parr Street, follow road round, turn left into Westfield Street. Cross

roundabout, continue down Westfield Street. Left into Eccleston Street, which becomes Knowsley Road.

Buses: 105, 121, 122 from Bickerstaffe Street in town centre. Limited on Sundays

Directions by car:

From east, west and south: M62 take junction 7, then A570 (St Helens link road) to town centre. At roundabout, turn left onto A58 (Westfield Street). Turn right into Dunriding Lane, at end of road turn left into Knowsley Road, ground is on left.

From north: M6 take junction 24, A58, then turn right onto A580. Take A570 towards town centre, then turn right onto A58, then as above.

The new stadium:

St Helens new stadium will be on Peasley Cross Lane, off the A570 (St Helens link road).

Tourist information:

Liverpool Tourist Information, Queens Square, Liverpool, Merseyside, L1 1RG. Tel.: 0151-709-3631. Fax: 0151-708-0204

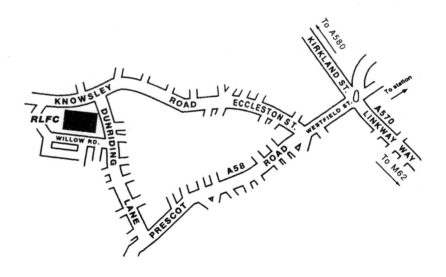

Salford City Reds

Ground: The Willows.
Address: The Pavilion, Willows Road, Weaste, Salford, M5 2FQ.
Telephone: 0161-736-6564. Commercial Dept.: 0161-661-1788
Lottery / pools office: 0161-281-5066
Fax: 0161 745 8072. Commercial Dept.: 0161-745-807.
Hotline: 0891 440016
Website: www.reds.co.uk
E-mail: info@reds.co.uk
Capacity: 11,500
Number of seats: 2,500

History of ground: The Willows has been home to Salford since 1901, when deadly local rivals Swinton were the first visitors. It is another ground that was adjacent to a cricket pitch (the cricket ground is alas, no more) and gets its name from the willow trees that are now hidden by the North Stand.

The record attendance of 26,470 was in 1937 when the original Red Devils played Warrington in a first round Challenge Cup tie. Floodlights were installed in 1966 and first used for the visit of Widnes. The ground has hosted two Challenge Cup Finals in 1904 and 1911, and Championship Finals in 1908 and 1909. It also staged two Test matches in 1922 and 1971. Salford originated as Cavendish RFC in Moss Side, Manchester (1873-4) and also played at Throstle Nest Weir (1875 -1877), Mile Field (1878-9) and New Barnes as Salford (1879 -1901).

Description of ground: There is small open terracing at the Willows end of the ground. The terracing at the other end is partially covered by the north stand (currently closed). The wings of the main stand have been rebuilt in recent years and would provide a clear view of the whole pitch but for the posts in the older, central section. The terraces on the east side are covered by an old stand.

Stands and terraces:
Restrictions on use: None.
Views from different areas: Main stand some obstruction by pillars.
Under cover: Main stand, terracing under north stand and terracing on east side.

Transfers to seats: Pay at turnstiles, then transfer in ground. There are no concessions for the main stand tickets.

Tickets for the high-level stands (above central stand) can only be bought as part of an executive package incorporating three-course meal, special car parking space, programme before the match and light refreshments afterward. VIP package is similar, but cheaper, and the ticket is for the main stand.

Entrance price reductions:
Children: Yes.

Senior citizens: Yes.

Students: Yes, with college, not NUS card.

There are no concessionary turnstiles – tickets must be bought from the ticket office on Willows Road.

Disabled: See below.

Family tickets or reductions: Contact club for details.

Club shop:
Club merchandise on sale from kiosk near club offices.

Opening hours: Office hours and match days.

Main items of stock: Shirts and souvenirs.

Supporters with disabilities:
Wheelchair access or designated area: Disabled supporters admitted free on application to the secretary's office at the Willows. Ramp provides access to covered area of south wing of the main stand. There are 8 wheelchair/companion places. Companions require a ground ticket from the ticket office at normal ground entrance price.

Other special facilities: None.

Disabled toilets: Main stand

Access to facilities (bars etc.): Some.

Designated car parking at ground: Must be reserved in advance - contact the club office.

Catering:
Three kiosks in the corners of the ground.

Main items on sale: Tea, coffee, burgers, pies, etc

Restaurant at ground: Yes.

Bars:
In The Willows Social Club, open before and after the game. No restrictions on use.

Facilities for activities for junior supporters: None.
Match day creche: None.
General facilities for hire: In The Willows Social Club.
Other sports at stadium: None.
Local facilities: Weaste Hotel, Edward Avenue

Car parking:
Secure car park at All Hallows School on Weaste Lane.
Street parking: Adequate near ground, streets immediately around ground restricted on match days. Ample parking off Weaste Lane.

Public transport:
Information: 0161-228-7811. Metrolink: 0161-205-2000
Metrolink: Manchester to Eccles service every 12-15 minutes on Sundays to Weaste station. There are also Metrolink stations at Manchester Piccadilly and Victoria train stations. Buses also serve Piccadilly and Eccles bus station. Ticket machines and route maps on station platforms.
From Eccles rail station: turn left down Church Street, left again at roundabout, to Metrolink station (or take a one-mile walk along Eccles New Road to Weaste).
From Salford Crescent rail station: cross road via subway and catch 67, 68 or 100 bus to Buile Hill Park/Weaste Lane.
Number 10 bus from Warrington bus station stops at church at Liverpool Street.
Number 33 bus from Wigan bus station stops near Weaste Metrolink station
If walking from Salford Shopping Centre bus station, cross car park from Pendleton Way side, turn right on Fitzwarren Street, first left along Lower Seedley Road and then bear right along Gore Avenue (¾ mile walk).

Directions by car:
From east or west: Take M62 to junction 12, then M602. At first junction, take first exit, A576. Turn right into Weaste Lane, B5228, and ground is on right.
From Manchester: Take A6 from city centre, turn left onto A576, then left into Weaste Lane, B5228, and ground is on right.

Tourist Information:
Manchester Visitor Centre, Town Hall Extension, Lloyd Street, Manchester, M60 2LA.
Tel.: 0161-234-3157/8. Fax: 0161-236-9900.

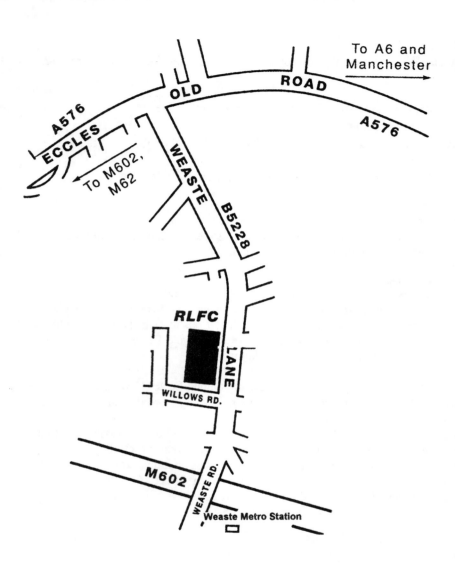

Sheffield Eagles

Ground: Don Valley Stadium
Address: Don Valley Stadium, Worksop Road, Sheffield, S9 3TL.
Telephone: 0114 261 0326
Fax: 0114 261 0303
Website: www.sheffieldeagles.com
E-mail: angie@sheffieldeagles.com
Capacity: 25,000
Number of seats: 25,000

History of ground: The Don Valley Stadium is now the established home of the Eagles and the club has recently celebrated ten years at the venue. The all-seater stadium holds 25,000, was built for the 1991 World Student Games, and opened in 1990. The club's record attendance is somewhat short of the 25,000 capacity at 10,603 when Bradford visited in August 1997. The club only use the main stand and with the running track play can seem somewhat distant compared to other grounds.

The Eagles started off at the Owlerton Greyhound (and speedway) Stadium in 1984 where a record attendance of 3,636 saw the Eagles lose to Oldham in a third round Challenge Cup game in 1989. The Eagles have also used Bramhall Lane, home of Sheffield United FC, where there was a record attendance of 8,636 for the visit of Widnes in 1989. The Eagles have also played at Hillsborough, home of Sheffield Wednesday FC, and various grounds in Yorkshire and Derbyshire when Don Valley has been unavailable.

Description of ground: Modern athletics stadium. Only main stand used for Eagles games. Good facilities, but can lack atmosphere due to distance from pitch and large numbers of empty seats in the rest of the stadium. The centre sections of the upper tier are reserved for season ticket holders.

Stands and terraces:
Restrictions on use: Centre sections reserved for season ticket holders.
Views from different areas: Good.
Under cover: All.
Transfers to seats: Not applicable.

Entrance price reductions:
Children: Yes (up to 16 years). *Disabled:* Yes.
Senior citizens: Yes. *Family tickets or reductions:* No,
Students: Yes. except for season tickets.

Club shop:
Kiosk on stadium concourse.
Opening hours: On matchdays. Monday to Friday 9am to 4.30pm.
Main items of stock: Shirts plus club souvenirs.

Supporters with disabilities:
Wheelchair access or designated area: Viewing area in main stand.
Other special facilities: Lifts.
Disabled toilets: Yes, main concourse near shop.
Access to facilities (bars etc.): Yes.
Designated car parking at ground: Yes.
Don Valley is one of the best stadiums for wheelchair access.

Catering:
Two kiosks on stadium concourse.
Main items on sale: One kiosk sells burgers, hot dogs etc., the other sells
beer and wine, both sell hot and cold drinks.
Restaurant at ground: Yes.

Bars:
On concourse in main stand.

Facilities for activities for junior supporters: Yes, bouncy castle, face
painting etc.
Match-day creche: No.
General facilities for hire: Contact stadium for details.
Other sports at stadium: Athletics and football.
Local facilities, pubs, cafes or restaurants: The Cocked Hat Pub and Fara
Pub by main entrance

Car parking:
Car park at ground for VIP/disabled only. Coleridge Road car park available
(Subject to other events), charge £1.00.
Street parking: Limited.

Public transport:
Information: 01709 515151 or 0114-272-8782
Nearest station: Sheffield (Midland Mainline).

From station, turn right along Sheaf Street, first left into Harmer Lane, then right into Pond Street past the bus station. Bear right to the top of the street to the Supertram stop at Fitzalan Square (Ponds Forge) on the far side of Commercial Street (¼ mile). Catch the Meadowhall service (every 10 minutes) to Attercliffe station. From Attercliffe station: turn right along Chippenham Street (¼ mile). Pay on tram. Return journey: catch Herdings Park or Middlewood service. Herdings Park service continues to train station.

(N.B. It is a shorter walk from the train station to the Supertram stop on the opposite side of the train station to the main entrance, but the service is every 20 minutes and the journey time is 18 minutes instead of 8 minutes.

From Meadowhall interchange: Any Supertram service to Don Valley stop, which is ¼ mile from stadium. Cross tracks, turn left and follow the path alongside line.
Buses: 8, 17, 69, 70, 130, 208, 225, 287, 289, 293, 296 and X2.

Directions by car:
From south: M1 junction 34, take A6178 into Sheffield. Stadium on left. Well signposted.
From east, west and north: M1 junction 34, take A6109 into Sheffield. Turn left into A6021 (Hawke St) and right onto A6178 (Attercliffe Common), and stadium is on left.
N.B. Junction 34 is used for the Meadowhall shopping centre, and therefore can be very busy.

Tourist Information:
1, Tudor Square, Sheffield, S. Yorkshire, S1 2HH.
Tel: 0114-273-4671/2. Fax: 0114-272-4225.
Email: enquiries@destinationsheffield.org.uk

The main stand at Don Valley Stadium

Swinton Lions

Ground: Gigg Lane.
Address: Bury Football Club, Gigg Lane, Bury BL9 9HR.
Club shop & lottery office: 112, Station Road, Swinton M27 6BT.
Telephone: 0161-761-2328 and 0161-705-2144.
Station Road: 0161-794-6150.
Fax: 0161-763-9196. Station Road: 0161-728-6174.
Website: swinton-lions-rlc.co.uk
E-mail: buryfc@dial.pipex.com
Capacity: 11,600
Number of seats: 11,600

History of ground: The Lions have played at Gigg Lane, Bury since their move from Station Road, Swinton in 1992. Bury Football Club have played here since they were founded in 1885. At one time the ground had a capacity of over 41,000, but its reduced all-seater capacity now is adequate for both the football and Rugby League clubs. One distinguishing mark in the ground's history is that it was the first in the north west to install floodlights.

The spiritual home of the club is Station Road, where they played from 1930. It was a large atmospheric ground which had a record attendance of 44,621 for a Challenge Cup semi-final replay in 1951. Floodlights were acquired with a loan from the RFL in 1964. At its height there were over 3,000 seats and the ground hosted five Championship Finals between 1965 and 1972 and 15 Test matches between 1930 and 1967. Swinton had previously played at a field in the Station Road area (1871-1887) and Chorley Road (1887-1929). The move to Bury came very suddenly in 1992, and the club lost a layer of support with the move. A housing estate was built on the old ground.

Description of ground:
A modernisation programme has produced a compact all-seater stadium with good facilities for both sports. All areas are under cover. The all-seater stadium hosted the Leigh versus Dewsbury Northern Ford Premiership Grand Final in July 2000, Dewsbury winning a thrilling match by one point. For Swinton's Rugby League matches, only the main stand is used, with

home fans in one section and away fans in another, directors and season ticket holders using the centre area.

Stands and terraces:
Restrictions on use: Home and away fans are segregated for some matches. Centre area of the stand is for season ticket holders.
Views from different areas: Good and unobstructed.
Under cover: All areas.
Transfers to seats: Not applicable.

Entrance price reductions:
Children: Yes.   *Disabled:* No.
Senior citizens: Yes.   *Family tickets or reductions:* No.
Students: No.

Club shop:
By main reception on match days. There is also a club shop in Station Road, Swinton.
Opening hours: Gigg Lane: match days. Station Road: office hours.
Main items of stock: Shirts, souvenirs, badges, mugs etc.

Supporters with disabilities:
Wheelchair access or designated area: Wheelchair area at front of main stand.
Other special facilities: None.
Disabled toilets: Yes - in main stand.
Access to facilities (bars etc.): No.
Designated car parking at ground: Yes - contact club for details.

Catering:
Kiosks in main stand.
Main items on sale: Burgers, hot dogs, tea & coffee, cold drinks.
Restaurant at ground: Pitch-side restaurant offering pre-match meal and match ticket etc..

Bars:
Social club outside ground. Also does food - burgers, sausages, chips, etc.

Facilities for activities for junior supporters: None.

Match-day creche: None.

General facilities for hire: Contact club for details.

Other sports at stadium: Football (Bury F.C.).

Local facilities, pubs, cafes or restaurants: No pubs in immediate area near ground. Social club.

Car parking:

No parking at ground.

Street parking: Immediate area restricted. Side street parking available. For bigger matches, try Redvales Road area off Manchester Road, south of ground, by playing fields.

Public transport:

Information: 0161-228-7811. Metrolink: 0161-205-2000

Nearest station: Bury (Metrolink). Trams from Manchester Piccadilly & Victoria train stations. Every 12 minutes. Ticket machines and route maps on station platforms. Journey time from Piccadilly or Victoria - between 20 and 25 minutes.

Buses: 135 from Manchester Piccadilly Gardens (3 per hour). Journey time: 40 minutes. From Bury bus station down Manchester Road: 135 (3 per hour), 524 (½ hourly) and 92 (hourly).

Directions by car:

From east or west: Take M62 to junction 17, then A56 (signposted Whitefield or Bury). Pass junction with A6053, and Gigg Lane is on right, opposite playing fields. Not well signposted.

From Bury Town Centre: Take A56, and Gigg Lane is on left.

(N.B. Ignore M66 which is signposted Bury from M62. Above route is more straightforward.)

Tourist Information:

Bury Tourist Information Centre, The Met Arts Centre, Market Street, Bury, Lancashire, BL9 0BN.

Tel.: 0161-253-5111. Fax.: 0161-253-5919.

Email: touristinformation@bury.gov.uk

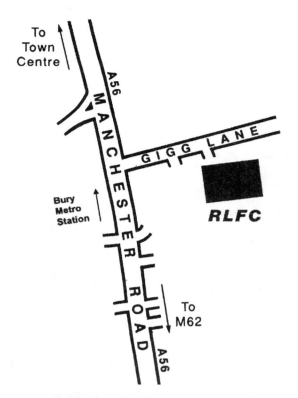

Leigh versus Dewsbury NFP Grand Final at Swinton July 2000

Wakefield Trinity Wildcats

Ground: Belle Vue.
Address: Belle Vue, Doncaster Road, Wakefield WF1 5HT.
Offices: Trinity House, 17 George Street, Wakefield WF1 1NE.
Telephone: Belle Vue & office: 01924 211611. Club shop: 01924-211711.
Clubcall: 0930-168876
Website: www.trinitywildcats.co.uk
Email: webmaster@trinitywildcats.co.uk
Capacity: 10,000
Number of seats: 1,600

History of ground: Belle Vue has been the home of Rugby League in the city since 1879. The ground hosted a record crowd of 37,676 in 1936 for a Challenge Cup semi-final. Floodlights were installed in 1967 and were first used for a Yorkshire versus Australia match and were upgraded in 1990-19911. Belle Vue also starred in the epic film *This Sporting Life*, when members of the crowd and cardboard replicas were used for filming at the match against Wigan in 1962 for a third round Challenge Cup game when the attendance was 28,254, not including the cardboard spectators. Trinity had previously played at Heath Common (1873), Manor Field (1875-6) and Elm Tree Street (1877). Belle Vue has hosted a Challenge Cup Final in 1923 and two Championship Finals in 1908 & 1930, and is the oldest current Rugby League ground in the UK.

Description of ground: Main stand on one side, open stand on opposite side, open terracing behind one goal, hospitality stand behind other goal. In need of modernising to bring up to Super League standard.

Stands and terraces:
Restrictions on use: None.
Views from different areas: Pillars obstruct view from main stand.
Under cover: Only main stand and hospitality area.
Transfers to seats: Pay at turnstile.

Entrance price reductions:
Children: Yes.   *Students:* No.
Senior citizens: Yes.   *Disabled:* Yes.

81

Family tickets or reductions: Contact club for details.

Club shop:
17 George Street, Wakefield WF1 1NE.
Opening hours: Office hours.
Match Day: In car park by turnstiles.
Main items of stock: Shirts, souvenirs, flags etc.

Supporters with disabilities:
Wheelchair access or designated area: No specific area.
Other special facilities: None.
Disabled toilets: No.
Access to facilities (bars etc.): Access to bar in hospitality suite.
Designated car parking at ground: No.

Catering:
Two kiosks opposite main stand.
Main items on sale: Burgers, hot dogs, hot and cold drinks.
Restaurant at ground: No, food in The Coach House, by main stand.

Bars:
In The Coach House on main stand side and in hospitality suite.

Facilities for activities for junior supporters: No.
Match-day creche: No.
General facilities for hire: Function rooms in new stand behind goal.
Other sports at stadium: Football (Emley FC), Health Club and bowling.
Local facilities, pubs, cafes or restaurants: Pub across road, Wimpy at superstore.

Car parking:
No parking at ground.
Street parking: Some in local streets. Some in Superbowl 2000 car park, also try Sugar Lane area near cemetery.

Public transport:
Information: 0113 245 7676 (buses).
Nearest station: Wakefield Westgate (mainline), Kirkgate. From Westgate station, turn left and immediately right into Quebec Street. This joins Ings Road, follow through to Doncaster Road, turn right and ground on right. Approximately 1 mile.

From Kirkgate: from Station Passage, turn left onto Doncaster Road and ground is ½ mile on right.

Buses: (Sundays - most hourly) 149, 150, 168, 185, 467,497.

Directions by car:

From west: M62 to junction 29, then M1 south to junction 41. Take A650, then A61 to town centre. After town centre, fork left onto A638, and ground is on right. To avoid M62/M1 junction, leave M62 at junction 28, take A653, then A650 to Wakefield.

From east: M62 take junction 30, A642 to town centre. Turn left at roundabout onto A61, then as for west above.

From north: M1 to junction 41, then as for west above.

From south: M1 to junction 39, take A636 signposted Wakefield. Turn right onto A638, then right onto A61, then as for west above.

Tourist Information:

Wakefield Tourist Information Centre, Town Hall, Wood Street, Wakefield, W. Yorkshire WF1 2HQ. Tel: 01924-305000. Fax: 01924-305775.

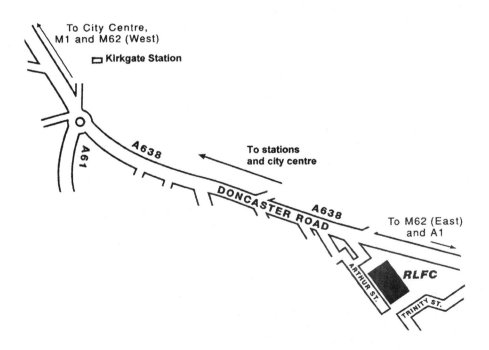

Warrington Wolves

Ground: Wilderspool Stadium.
Address: Wilderspool Stadium, Fletcher Street, Warrington WA4 6PY.
Telephone: 01925-635338; Club shop / ticket office: 01925-235005; Touchdown club: 01925-634903.
Fax: 01925-571744
Website: www.warringtonwolves.com
E-mail: info@wwrlfc.co.uk
Capacity: 9,561
Number of seats: 2,065

History of ground: Wilderspool has been the home of Warrington since 1898. The record attendance is 34,304 for a league match against local rivals Wigan in 1949. The Brian Bevan stand, honouring the club's most famous player, was built in 1983 after the old main stand had been gutted by fire in 1982 causing £300,000 worth of damage. The ground had the honour of being the first BBC2 Rugby League transmission in 1965 when Warrington played Widnes, which was only shown in the South of England. The ground has hosted two Championship Finals in 1927 and 1934, and one Test Match in 1973. It also staged the classic 1995 World Cup match between New Zealand and Tonga, the Kiwis winning with an injury time drop goal. Warrington previously played on several minor grounds in the locality between 1879 and 1898.

The club are now planning to move to a new ground in the town, as there is not enough room at the cramped Wilderspool site to develop a modern stadium. So another of the sport's great historic venues will be lost.

Description of ground: A combination of the new and the old - the modern main stand provides good unobstructed views from the seats and has a terrace enclosure in front. The south side of the ground has not been used for four seasons. The club has carried out safety works and the terrace will re-open during the 2001 season. This area will become the family enclosure and will increase the ground capacity by 500. There are covered terraces behind both goals. The Fletcher Street end is used mainly by home supporters and the Railway end by away fans. Look out for the Brian Bevan statue at the roundabout just north of the ground.

Stands and terraces:
Restrictions on use: None, but no changing ends at half time on the terraces.
Views from different areas: Generally good views. Unobstructed in main stand. Both terraces behind the goals have pillars.
Under cover: Both ends and Brian Bevan stand.
Transfers to seats: No transfers inside ground. Buy seat tickets at ticket office on Fletcher Street.

Entrance price reductions:
Children: Yes.
Senior citizens: Yes.
Students: Yes.

Disabled: Yes
Family tickets or reductions: No.

Club shop:
Outside ground in Fletcher Street. Inside ground at Fletcher Street end.
Opening hours: Monday - Saturday 9-5; matchdays 3 hours before kick-off, ½ hour after
Main items of stock: Shirts, polo shirts, fleeces, sweatshirts. caps, videos, flags scarves etc.

Supporters with disabilities:
Wheelchair access or designated area: Front of Fletcher Street terracing.
Other special facilities: None.
Disabled toilets: Fletcher Street end.
Access to facilities: Limited.
Designated car parking at ground: Some disabled parking spaces in Priory Street car park, first come first served. Contact club for details.

Catering:
At ends of ground on terracing and in stand.
Main items on sale: Burgers, pies, hot dogs, peas, hot and cold drinks, confectionery.
Restaurant at ground: Yes, places need to be booked in advance.

Bars:
In main stand and kiosks on terracing.

Facilities for activities for junior supporters: Junior activities organised through the Wolfpack.

Match-day creche: None.

General facilities for hire: Touchdown club, function room, Platinum club and vice-presidents club.

Other sports at stadium: None.

Local facilities: The Causeway, corner of Causeway Avenue and Wilderspool Way, The Waterside (Park Boulevard) and other local pubs.

Car parking:

Parking at ground: St James Car Park off roundabout at Brian Bevan statue, there is a £2 charge. Manweb car park for permit holders. Town centre parking in Mersey Street.

Street parking: Some a few minutes walk from ground.

Public transport:

Information: 0151-236-7676.

Train: Warrington Bank Quay station. ¾ mile walk to ground. Bear right along Wilson Patten Street. Turn right at traffic lights over the Mersey, and right at roundabout onto Wilderspool Causeway. Bear left at Brian Bevan Island, past St James' Church and turn left into Fletcher Street.

Warrington Central station. ¾ mile walk to ground. Turn left along Winwick Street, and walk through the shopping precinct. Cross over the Mersey, then as above.

Buses: 5, 6, 7, 8, 9, 43, 44, 45, 46, 62, 65.

From Golden Square bus station: ¾ mile walk to ground. Turn right along Golborne Street, turn right at the traffic lights into Winwick Street, then as above.

Directions by car:

From north, east or west: M62 to junction 9, then A49 signposted Warrington. Stay on A49, which becomes Wilderspool Causeway, and ground is on left.

From south: M6 junction 20, take M56 west. At junction 10 take A49 signposted Warrington. This becomes Wilderspool Causeway, and ground is on right.

From north Wales: M56 junction 11. Turn left at roundabout onto A56. This leads to Brian Bevan Island - turn left for ground.

Tourist Information:

Warrington Tourist Information Centre, 21, Rylands Street, Warrington, Cheshire, WA1 1EJ.

Tel.: 01925-442180. Fax: 01925-442149.

Email: informationcentre@warrington.gov.uk

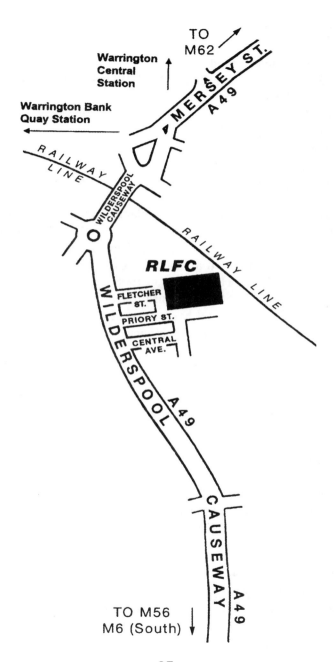

Whitehaven

Ground: Recreation Ground
Address: Recreation Ground, Coach Road, Whitehaven, CA28 9DD.
Telephone: 01946-692915
Fax: 01946-695805
Website: www.marras.co.uk
E-mail: None
Capacity: 6,000
Number of seats: 550

History of ground: Whitehaven were admitted into the Rugby League in 1948 and there first game was against Hull on the 21 August before 15,000 fans. The Recreation Ground had been used for junior games since the turn of the century and had hosted a Challenge Cup game when the then junior side had beaten mighty St Helens 13-8 in 1908 before 2,000 spectators. The record attendance was 18,500 for a third round Challenge Cup game versus Wakefield in 1960. The ground has witnessed many other sports including football, boxing, speedway and whippet racing.

Description of ground: Excellent ground for viewing, as all areas are close to the action and have good elevated positions. No additional charge for grandstand seats is an excellent initiative, and compensates for lack of cover on the 'popular side' terracing. The modern grandstand has easy access and is clean and comfortable. There is a covered terrace behind one goal.

Stands and terraces:
Restrictions on use: None.
Views from different areas: Clear views, close to pitch from all four sides. Terracing on three sides. Slight pillar obstructions in covered terracing.
Under cover: Grandstand and one end.
Transfers to seats: Free.

Entrance price reductions:
Children: Yes (up to age 16)
Senior citizens: Yes.
Students: Yes.
Disabled: Contact club for details.

Family tickets or reductions: Free admission for members of Young Supporters Club.

Club shop: Inside ground, at back of covered terrace.
Opening hours: Matchdays plus Saturdays and Sundays between 10.00a.m. and 1.00p.m.
Main items of stock: Replica shirts, jackets, hats, baseball caps, confectionery, crisps, hot & cold drinks.

Supporters with disabilities:
Wheelchair access or designated area: Yes, viewing area in front of main stand. Access by arrangement.
Other special facilities: No.
Disabled toilets: Yes. By main entrance.
Access to facilities (bars etc.): Yes.
Designated car parking at ground: Yes. By arrangement.

Catering:
One small van, inside ground. Also tea and coffee etc in Supporters Club Shop at back of covered terrace. More facilities provided for major matches.
Main items on sale: Burgers, hot dogs, hot drinks.
Restaurant at ground: None.

Bars: Avon Bar. Inside ground open from 1.00p.m. on matchdays. No restrictions.

Facilities for activities for junior supporters: Young Supporters Club.
Match-day creche: Free facilities on match days.
General facilities for hire: Avon bar available for functions.
Other sports at stadium: None
Local facilities, pubs, cafes or restaurants: Pubs: The Castle at top of coach road, Ginns pub at opposite end of Coach road, near to parking. MacDonalds nearby on Flatts Walks.

Car parking:
Parking at ground: Yes.
Street parking: Limited in immediate area around ground. Free parking at nearby Ginns car park.

Public transport:
Nearest station: Corkickle Station (closed Sundays and evenings, infrequent service). Whitehaven station (limited service from Carlisle, only).

Buses: Information 0870-6082608. Stops on Inkerman Terrace or to Corkickle station.

Directions by car:
M6 take junction 40, A66 signposted Keswick. After passing Keswick and Cockermouth, turn left onto A595. Stay on A595, pass first junction with A5094. Turn right at traffic lights into A5094 (Inkerman Terrace), left into Coach Road, and ground is on left. NB A66 maybe be busy in summer, and has very little dual carriageway.

Tourist Information: Whitehaven Tourist Information Centre, Market Hall, Market Place, Whitehaven, Cumbria CA28 7JG. Tel: 01946-852954.
Website: www.thebeacon@copelandbc.gov.uk.

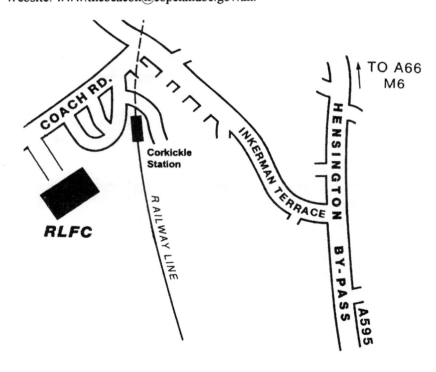

Widnes Vikings

Ground: Autoquest Stadium.
Address: Autoquest Stadium, Lowerhouse Lane, Widnes WA8 7DZ.
Telephone: 0151-420-0054.
Fax: 0151-423-2720
Website: www.widnes-vikings.com
E-mail: None
Capacity: 10,883
Number of seats: 10,883

History of ground: The Autoquest Stadium has been the home of the club since 1884, when it was called Naughton Park. Widnes previously played at various local grounds from 1873-1884. The record attendance at the re-vamped stadium was 6,644 for a Northern Ford Premiership game against Leigh on Boxing Day, 2000. The initial arrangement was for the Rugby League club to be part owners of the stadium, but in 1999, the club gave up its 40% shareholding in favour of tenancy agreement. Prior to the redevelopment, the record attendance was for a first round replay Challenge Cup against St Helens in 1965 when 24,205 attended.

Before the redevelopment, the ramshackle nature of the ground was offset by the great atmosphere. Floodlights were installed in 1965, and the first floodlit match was the league visit by St Helens which attracted an attendance of 17,319. The ground staged a World Cup quarter-final between Wales and Papua New Guinea in 2000, and in 1998 an Emerging England team played Wales.

Description of ground: The redevelopment of the ground, funded by selling it to the local Council and through a Sport England grant, has seen its complete modernisation, while allowing the club to remain at its traditional home. There are three cantilever stands, with the east end still undeveloped. A stadium is suitable for Super League, but to fully use it the club must regain the place in the top flight that it lost in 1995 with the restructuring that followed the introduction of Super League. Only the north and south stands are usually used for Rugby League matches.

Stands and terraces:
Restrictions on use: None.

Views from different areas: All unobstructed.

Under cover: All areas.

Transfers to seats: Not applicable, but there are no transfers between the north and south stands in the ground.

Entrance price reductions:

Children: Yes.

Senior citizens: Yes.

Students: Yes.

Disabled: Yes.

Family tickets or reductions: No.

Club shop:

By ticket office in south stand.

Opening hours: Office hours and match days.

Main items of stock: Shirts and souvenirs. Also have some Everton F.C. items as their reserve team play at the stadium.

Supporters with disabilities:

Wheelchair access or designated area: Wheelchair area at front of north/west stand.

Other special facilities: None.

Disabled toilets: South, north and west stands.

Access to facilities (bars etc.): In stand.

Designated car parking at ground: Contact club.

Catering:

Kiosks in north, west and south stands.

Main items on sale: Beer, hot & cold drinks, burgers, pasties, sausage rolls, sweets, etc.

Restaurant at ground: Yes.

Bars:

In south stand and in ground.

Facilities for activities for junior supporters: No.

Match-day creche: Yes, if required.

General facilities for hire: Function rooms available at stadium.

Other sports at stadium: Football (Everton reserves).

Local facilities, pubs, cafes or restaurants: None in immediate area.

Car parking:
Parking at ground - ticket only.
Street parking: Some and car parks near the ground all free.

Public transport:
Information: 0151-236-7676 or 0151-423-3333 (buses).
Nearest station: Widnes North. From station, turn right into Birchfields Road, continue along Kingsway, then right into Sinclair Avenue. (1 mile)
Buses: 5 and 14 on Sundays.

Directions by car:
From north, east or west: M62 take junction 7, then A568. Stay on A568 bypassing town centre, and come off onto A562 (Ashley Way). Go straight across two roundabouts into Lower House Lane, and ground is on right.
From south: M6 junction 20, M56 west. M56 junction 12 take A557 signposted Runcorn and Widnes. Join A533 signposted Widnes, cross Runcorn Bridge, then turn off onto A562. Then as above.

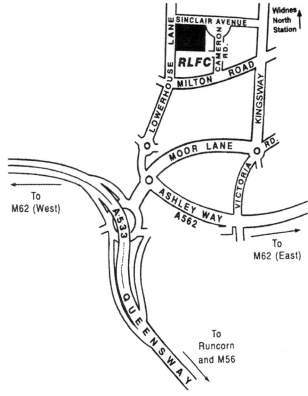

Tourist Information:
Liverpool Tourist Information, Queen Square, Liverpool, Merseyside, L1 1RG.
Tel: 0151-709-3631.
Fax: 0151-708-0204.

Wigan Warriors

Ground: JJB Stadium.
Address: JJB Stadium, Loire Drive, Wigan, WN5 0UZ.
Telephone: 01942 774000. **Ticketline:** 08451 473227.
Fax: 01942 214880.
Website: www.wiganrl.com
Email: wrlfc@jjb.stadium.co.uk
Capacity: 25,032
Seats: 25,032

History of ground: The JJB Stadium has been Wigan's home since 1999 when the Warriors played a top-five play-off there against Castleford. Selling Central Park was a huge change for the club, and it will take some time before the JJB Stadium really feels like home. Ironically, the next major match after Wigan's first game involved local rivals St Helens in the World Club Challenge against Melbourne Storm.

Central Park was the home of the game in the town from 1902 and was one the most famous venues for sport in Britain. The record attendance at the ground was 47,747 for a league game against St Helens in 1949, which is also the record attendance for a league game in Britain. The ground also hosted the Challenge Cup Final in 1927, 1928 and 1932 and five Championship Finals between 1931 and 1975. The stadium also hosted eighteen test matches between 1926 and 1989, and a World Cup match in 1995. Wigan had previously played at five other grounds, including Springfield Park (1901-2), between 1876 and 1902.

Description of ground: Modern stadium with good views and facilities, but still feels anodyne compared to Central Park. Some work to show it is a Rugby League stadium would help - why not name a couple of the stands after Wigan Rugby League players?

Stands and terraces:
Restrictions on use: Visiting support in north stand.
Views from different areas: All stands cantilevered, so all have clear views.
Under cover: All stands are under cover.
Transfers to seats: Not applicable. No transfers within ground.

Entrance price reductions:
Children: Yes. Also "Quid a Kid" vouchers accepted. Kelvinz Klub - child season ticket for home and away matches.
Senior citizens: Yes.

Students: No.
Disabled: Contact club.
Family tickets or reductions: For season tickets.

Club shop:
In JJB Soccer Dome.
Opening hours: Office hours and match days.
Main items of stock: JJB sports store with a few Wigan RL souvenirs; replica shirts etc.

Supporters with disabilities:
Wheelchair access or designated area: Yes, in all stands.
Other special facilities: For visually impaired.
Disabled toilets: Lower west stand, Lower north stand.
Access to facilities: Not to kiosks on concourse.
Designated car parking at ground: Limited number of places at ground. Contact club for details.

Catering:
Kiosks in all stands.
Main items on sale: Pies, hot dogs, tea and coffee.
Restaurant at ground: Yes. Also hamburger restaurant in JJB Soccerdome.

Bars:
In all stands.

Facilities for activities for junior supporters: Five-a-side soccer in JJB Soccerdome. Rugby league match-day activities organised by Kelvinz Klub.
Match-day creche: None.
General facilities for hire: Lounges and suites. Contact club for details.
Other sports at stadium: Football (Wigan Athletic FC). Athletics stadium next door to stadium. Five-a-side football in JJB Soccerdome.
Local facilities: Various pubs and restaurants in immediate area.

Car parking:
Plenty of parking at the ground, adequate for most matches. Can be slow to clear afterwards. N.B. Sign to M6 by exit past Soccerdome is for the north.
Street parking: Restrictions on side roads on match days. Limited near ground. Alternative is to park in the town centre and walk to the ground.

Public transport:
Information: 0161-228-7811
Train: From Wigan North Western station: turn left onto Wallgate, follow road for approximately 1 mile and turn right into Robin Park Road. Stadium on right past ASDA supermarket. Approximately 1½ miles.
From Wigan Wallgate station: turn right onto Wallgate, then as above.
Buses: All buses from Wigan North Western station go towards ground.

Directions by car: *From south:* M6 junction 25. A49 towards Wigan. At junction with A57, then A577, Robin Park Road is on left. *From north:* M6 junction 26, A577 towards Wigan, then left into Robin park Road at junction with A49. Ground is well signposted.

Tourist information:
Wigan Tourist Information Office, Trencherfield Mill, Wallgate, Wigan, Lancashire, WN3 4EL.
Tel: 01942-825677. Fax: 01942-825677.
Email: infounit@wiganmbc.gov.uk

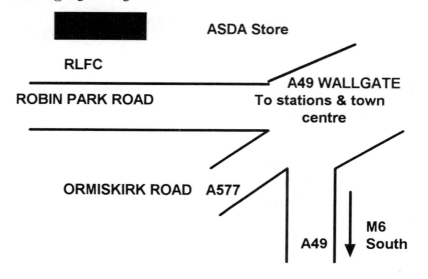

Workington Town

Ground: Derwent Park.
Address: Derwent Park, Bridge Street, Workington, Cumbria CA14 2HG.
Telephone: 01900-603609 (9.00a.m. to 3.00p.m. Monday to Thursday, 9.00a.m. to 2.00p.m. Friday).
Fax: 01900-871103
Website: www.workington-town.net
E-mail: None
Capacity: 10,000
Number of seats: 1,200

History of ground: Workington Town were admitted into the League in 1945. The club originally played at Borough Park home of Workington F.C., which is next door to Derwent Park, which was opened in 1956. Town won the League and the Challenge Cup while at Borough Park. There was a club record attendance of 20,403 for the game against St Helens for a third round Challenge Cup game in 1952. The record attendance for Derwent Park is 17,741 for a third round Challenge Cup game in 1965 against Wigan.

Floodlights were installed in 1990, and first used for a Cumbria versus Australia game. The club staged the Samoa versus Maori game in the 2000 World Cup.

Description of ground: The main stand and enclosure on one side and covered terrace on the other are adequate for the club's current needs. But the ground is in need of modernisation, either for a higher level of Rugby League, or for speedway, which attracts good attendances in the summer.

Stands and terraces:
Restrictions on use: None.
Views from different areas: Slight obstruction by pillars.
Under cover: Stand and terracing at side of pitch.
Transfers to seats: Pay at turnstile, no transfers in ground.

Entrance price reductions:
Children: Yes.
Senior citizens: Yes.
Students: No.

Disabled: Yes.
Family tickets or reductions: Yes.

Club shop:
None.
Opening hours: Not applicable
Main items of stock: Not applicable

Supporters with disabilities:
Wheelchair access or designated area: Wheelchair viewing area in front of main stand. Wheelchair users must be accompanied by an escort.
Other special facilities: None.
Disabled toilets: In main stand.
Access to facilities (bars etc.): Yes.
Designated car parking at ground: Contact club.

Catering:
2 burger vans in stadium.
Main items on sale: Burgers, chips, tea & coffee, crisps, some chocolate items.
Restaurant at ground: No

Bars:
Derwent Lounge / Gus Risman bar under main stand. No access to bars from within the ground.

Facilities for activities for junior supporters: None.
Match-day creche: None.
General facilities for hire: Derwent Lounge available for functions.
Other sports at stadium: Speedway.
Local facilities, pubs, cafes or restaurants: None in immediate area.

Car parking:
Plenty of parking at ground.
Street parking: None in immediate area.

Public transport:
Information: Buses: 01946-63222 (Stagecoach)
Nearest station: Workington - 100 yards from stadium.
Buses: Bus station is 10 minutes walk from ground.

Directions by car:
M6 take junction 40, A66 signposted Keswick. After passing Keswick and

Cockermouth, enter Workington. Turn right onto A596 (Bridge Street), and then right onto A597, New Bridge Road,(signposted Town Centre), pass Workington Football Club on left, go straight over roundabout, and ground is on right. Follow one way system, pass station and entrance is on left.

N.B. The A66 may be very busy during the summer, and very little of it is dual carriageway.

Tourist Information:
Workington Tourist Information Centre, Carnegie Arts Centre Theatre (Foyer), Finkle Street, Workington CA14 2BD.
Tel: 01900-602923.
Email: tourism@allerdale.gov.uk

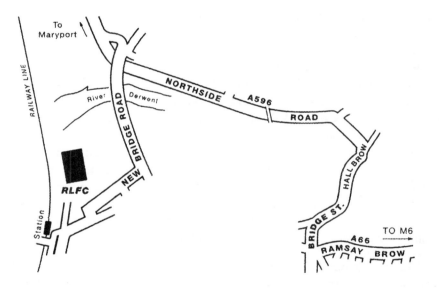

York Wasps

Ground: Huntingdon Stadium.
Address: Huntingdon Stadium, Jockey Lane, Huntingdon,
York, YO32 9XX.
Telephone: 01904-634636
Fax: 01904-629049
Website: None
E-mail: None
Capacity: 5,000
Number of seats: 800

History of ground: The Huntingdon (formerly Ryedale) Stadium has been home of York since 1989. The club's record attendance at this ground is 4,977 for the visit of Halifax for a league game in 1990. The floodlights were first used against Huddersfield in October 1989.

York previously played at Clarence Street from 1885 until 1989. The record attendance there was 14,631 for the visit of Swinton in a Challenge Cup first round game in 1934. York previously played at Knavesmire and at Poad's Field in the 1880s.

Faced with a large bill for safety work, York sold their traditional home in 1989. Plans to ground-share with York City F.C. broke down, and the club moved to their present home. Although the facilities are adequate for Northern Ford Premiership matches, the ground is three miles outside the city, with no public transport links. The athletics track also reduces the atmosphere even with a reasonable size crowd in the ground.

Description of ground: Modern athletics stadium, with a cantilever stand on one side and covered terracing on the other side. Adequate for the club's present needs.

Stands and terraces:
Restrictions on use: None.
Views from different areas: Unobstructed, except front four rows of stand are obstructed by dugouts by the pitch.
Under cover: Yes.
Transfers to seats: In ground.

Entrance price reductions:

Children: Yes.

Senior citizens: Yes.

Students: No.

Disabled: No.

Family tickets or reductions: No.

Club shop:
Some items available from club office.
Opening hours: Office hours.
Main items of stock: Shirts, scarves and hats.

Supporters with disabilities:
Wheelchair access or designated area: Yes - front of main stand.
Other special facilities: None.
Disabled toilets: Yes - in ladies and gentlemen's toilets under main stand.
Access to facilities (bars etc.): Yes to refreshment kiosks.
Designated car parking at ground: No.

Catering:
In main stand.
Main items on sale: Hot dogs, tea & coffee, soup, crisps, confectionery.
Restaurant at ground: Yes

Bars:
Behind main stand (entrance through leisure centre.) No access from ground during match.

Facilities for activities for junior supporters: No.
Match-day creche: No.
General facilities for hire: Leisure centre at stadium.
Other sports at stadium: Athletics. Swimming pool nearby.
Local facilities, pubs, cafes or restaurants: None in immediate area. A couple of pubs on way to ground from ring road.

Car parking:
Plenty of parking at ground.
Street parking: Limited.

Public transport:
Information: 01904-554488 (tourist information).
Nearest station: York. 3 miles away - taxi.

Buses: None.

Directions by car:
From south and west: A1 then A64 towards York. Stay on the A64, (ignore first sign for A1237) and at roundabout with A1237, take A1237. Immediately at roundabout, turn onto A1036 towards York. At roundabout turn right into Jockey Lane, left at next roundabout, and left into Kathryn Avenue for stadium. There are no signs for the stadium, follow signs for Monks Cross.

From north: A1, turn onto A1237, then as above. N.B. A1237 is not dual carriageway, and may be busy during the summer.

Tourist Information:
York Tourist Information Centre, 20, George Hudson Street, York, N. Yorkshire, YO1 2HB.
Tel: 01904-554488. Fax: 01904-554491.

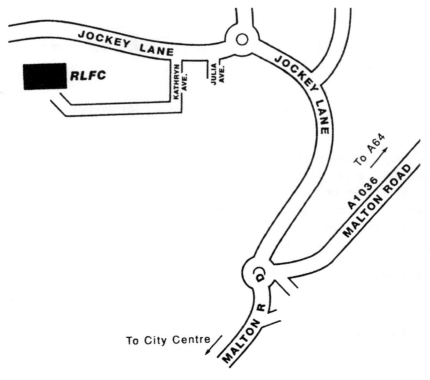

Banners at Wilderspool - March 2000

Ground sharing - Rugby League and football at Leigh's Hilton Park

Up for the Cup. Whitehaven supporters before the Challenge Cup match
against St Helens - February 2001

Other British Rugby League venues

There seems to be an almost endless variety of grounds that Rugby League matches are staged on these days. Below are some that we believe will be used regularly in the future, but with a wide selection of rugby union and football grounds available, almost anywhere is possible.

Old Trafford

Address: Old Trafford Stadium. Sir Matt Busby Way, Manchester M16 0RA
Telephone: 0161-872-1661 and 0161-930-1968
Station: Old Trafford (Metrolink) to & from Manchester City centre
Buses: 252-257 (inclusive), 17, 114 and 236 from Piccadilly
Directions by car: From North: Leave M60 at J12 for M602. At end of M602 (J3) follow signs for Salford Quays and Trafford Park. At roundabout turn right into Trafford Road (A5063). At bridge over Manchester Ship Canal keep to the right and follow signs. From South: Leave M6 at J19, take A56 in direction of Manchester Airport, pass the airport and follow signs to M60. Leave M60 at J7 following signs for Manchester United.
Other information: A lot of parking available in the vicinity of the ground, but expect to pay at least £5.

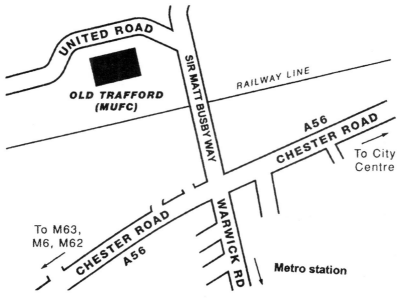

Twickenham

Address: Rugby Road, Twickenham, Middlesex, TW1 1DZ.
Telephone: 020-8892-8161
Station: Twickenham. ¼ mile walk to the stadium. Richmond (Rail and London Underground) shuttle buses on matchdays.
Buses: Information from 020-7222-1234
Directions: M25 to M3 then A316. From M1 take M25 then M3 towards Sunbury, at Sunbury the M3 becomes A316 follow signs for Richmond/central London not Twickenham. This is longer than using the North and South Circulars, but beyond Hanger Lane they can have very heavy traffic.
Other information: Parking at Stadium, but book for big matches. Street parking restrictions rigorously enforced. The Rugby Museum is worth a visit.

Murrayfield

Address: Murrayfield Rugby Stadium, Roseburn Street, Edinburgh EH12 5PJ
Telephone: 0131-346-5000
Station: Edinburgh Waverley then shuttle bus, or local trains to Haymarket and ½mile walk to the ground.
Buses: Information: 0131-554-4494
Directions: Murrayfield is west of the city centre. From west end of princes Street, head west and fork right at Haymarket station. Parking is restricted near ground for big matches, and travel by public transport may be advisable.

Millennium Stadium

Address: Westgate, Cardiff CF10 1JA
Telephone: 02920-68523961
Station: Cardiff Central - less than ¼ mile walk
Buses: Bus station by railway station
Directions: From the west leave the M4 at J31 and follow signs for Cardiff City centre. From the east, leave M4 at J29 taking the A48(M) into Cardiff city centre.
Other information: Quite a lot of parking in the city centre, but allow a lot of time to get there and to get into the stadium, as the entrances are quite spread out.

Wrexham Football Club

Address: Racecourse Ground, Mold Road, Wrexham, Clwyd LL11 2AH
Telephone: 01978-262129
Station: Wrexham General. Less than ¼mile from ground along Mold Road.
Buses: From stand 5 at King Street bus station.

Directions: From north and east: Take M56 to Chester and follow signs for Wrexham on M53 and A55. Leave the A55 and follow the A483 signposted Wrexham. From south and west: follow M54 to Shrewsbury, then A5 to Oswestry, then A483 signposted Wrexham. The ground is on Mold Road, the A541, which is off the A483.

Windsor Park, Belfast

Address: Donegall Avenue, Belfast BT12 6LW
Telephone: 02890-244198
Station: Adelaide station
Directions: Junction 1 of M1 motorway. Ground is between Boucher Road and Lisburn Road.

Tolka Park, Dublin

Address: Richmond Road, Dublin
Telephone: 00-3531-837-5754
Railway Station: Connolly Station Around 1 mile.
Buses: Any along Drumcondra Road.
Directions: Tolka Park is to the north of the city centre, in the Drumcondra district. Richmond Road is off Drumcondra Road, at the junction of Drumcondra Road Lower and Drumcondra Road Upper.

Partick Thistle FC

Address: 80 Firhill Road, Glasgow G20 7AL
Telephone: 0141-579-1971
Railway Station: Glasgow Queen Street. Underground: George's Cross and Kelvinbridge are around ½mile from the ground.
Directions: From city centre, A81 (Garscube Road) north. Firhill Road on right.

Richmond Athletic Ground

Address: Twickenham Road, Richmond, Surrey
Telephone: 020-8940-0397.
Station: Richmond, less than ¼ mile walk.
Buses: Information: 020-7222-1234.
Directions: Follow directions for Twickenham stadium (above) continue along A316 for further 1.5 miles north, cross Thames at Twickenham Bridge until Old Deer Park on left. Ground visible from A316.
Other information: Parking on the opposite side of the A316, free after 6.30 p.m.

Supporting the Bulls - Odsal April 2000

Supporting the Wolves -Wilderspool March 2000

BARLA National Conference Clubs

Ground addresses and telephone numbers.

Askam
Fallowfield Park, Sandy Lane, Askam-in-Furness. 01229-463320.

Blackbrook
Boardman's Lane, St Helens. 01744-603399.

Castleford Lock Lane
Hicksons Stadium, Lock Lane, Castleford. 01977-510200.

Castleford Panthers
Three Lane End Playing Fields, Raglan Close, Castleford 01977-513309.

Cottingham Tigers
Hill Top Sports & Social Club, Hull. 01482-671306.

Dewsbury Moor
229, Heckmondwike Road, Dewsbury. 01924-402283.

Dudley Hill
Neil Hunt Memorial Ground, Parry Lane, Bradford. 01274-669276.

East Leeds
Richmond Hill, Easy Road, Leeds. O113-293 0547.

Eastmoor Dragons
King George V Playing Fields, Woodhouse Road, Eastmoor, Wakefield. 01924-375367.

Eccles
Hallsworth Road, Off Schofield Road, Eccles. 0161-788-0011.

Featherstone Lions
Mill Pond Stadium, Wakefield Road, Featherstone. 01977-790278.

Heworth
The Clubhouse, Elm Park Way, York Y02. 01904-421075.

Hull Dockers
Tower Grange, Willows, Holderness Road, Hull. 01482-376404.

Ideal Isberg
County Ground, County Road North, North Hull. 01482-343852.

Keighley Albion
Crossflatts Cricket Club, near Bingley. 01274 562050.

Leigh East
Grasmere Street, Leigh. (next door to Hilton Park). 01942-608704.

Leigh Miners Rangers
Twist Lane, Leigh. 01942-672984.

London Skolars
New River Sports Stadium, White Hart Lane, London. 020-8889-1050

Milford Marlins
Becketts Park, Queenswood Drive, Leeds. 0113-2263030

Millom
Devonshire Field, Coronation Road, Millom. 01229-772030.

New Earswick All Blacks
New Earswick Sports Ground, White Rose Ave, York. 01904-492481.

Normanton Knights
Queen Elizabeth Drive, Normanton. 01924-897081.

Oldham St. Annes
Higginshaw Road, Oldham. 0161-678-8660.

Oulton Raiders
Raider Park, Oulton Green, Woodlesford, Leeds. 0113-2822356

Redhill
Carlyle Road, Airedale, Castleford. 01977-512958.

Rochdale Mayfield
Keswick Street, Castleton, Rochdale. 01706-527160

Saddleworth Rangers
Shawhall Bank Road, Greenfield, Oldham. 01457-876077

Shaw Cross Sharks
Grange Road, Shaw Cross, Dewsbury. 01924-463987.

Sheffield Hillsborough Hawks
Hillsborough Sports Arena, Sheffield. 0114-233-5310.

Siddal
Chevinedge, Jubilee Road, Halifax. 01422-367376

Skirlaugh
BP Chemicals Sports & Social Club, Salton End, Hedon, Hull. 01482-896113.

Thatto Heath
West Park RUFC, Prescot Road, St Helens. 01744-26138

Thornhill Trojans
Overthorpe Park, Thornhill, Dewsbury. 01924-464164

Walney Central
Central Park, Central Drive, Barrow-in-Furness. 01229-473826.

Waterhead
Waterhead Park, Peach Road, Oldham. 0161-624-9312.

West Bowling
Bankfoot Cricket Club, Stadium
Road, Bradford.
01274-679619.

West Hull
Hull RLFC, The Boulevard, Hull
01482-327200.

Wigan St. Judes
Parsons Meadow, Keats Avenue,
Wigan.
01942-826808.

Wigan St. Patricks
Clarington Park, Harper St,
Wigan.
01942-495071.

Woolston Rovers
Bennett's Recreation Ground,
Padgate, Warrington.
01925-812007

York Acorn
Acorn Sports & Social Club,
Thanet Road, York. 01904-330351.

For further information about
National Conference matches,
contact:
BARLA
West Yorkshire House,
4, New North Parade, Huddersfield
HD1 5JP.
Telephone: 01484-544131.
Fax: 01484-519985.

Woolston Rovers versus Leigh Miners Rangers - January 2000

Dropping in for the game - parachutist at Hull August 2000

About to kick off - Featherstone Rovers versus Barrow Border Raiders
January 2000

Rugby League Conference

Ground addresses; telephone numbers for ground or club official.

Bedford Swifts
Bedford Swifts RUFC
Bedford Athletics Stadium
Barkers Lane
Bedford, MK41 9SA
07860-454925

Birmingham Bulldogs
Moor Lane Sports Ground
Moor Lane, Witton
Birmingham B6 7AA
0121-356-1232

Bridlington Bulls
Bridlington RUFC
Dukes Park, Queensland
Bridlington, YO16 7LN
01262-676405

Cambridge Eagles
Cambridge RUFC
Granchester Road
Cambridge, CB3 9ED
07774-461708

Cardiff Demons
Cardiff Harlequins
Newport Road
Cardiff. 07748-140613

Chester Wolves
Chester RUFC
Hare Lane, Vicars Cross
Chester
01244-336017

Coventry Bears
Coventry RUFC
Barkers Butts Lane
Coventry, CV6 1DU
07956-251379

Crawley Jets
Willoughby Fields
Ifield Avenue
Ifield, Crawley
07973-211596

Crewe Wolves
Sandbach RUFC
Bradwell Road
Sandbach
07801-969246

Derby City
Moorways Sports Complex
Moor Lane, Allerton
Derby, DE24 9HY
07808-096361

Gloucestershire Warriors
Chosen Hill Former Pupils RUFC
Brookfield Road, Churchdown
Gloucestershire, GL3 2PP
07775-682353

Hemel Hempstead Stags
Pennine Way
Hemel Hempstead, HP2 5UD
07801-849471

113

Ipswich Rhinos
Ipswich RUFC
Humber Doucy Lane
Ipswich. 07860-876782

Kingston Warriors
Oaken Lane
Claygate, Surrey
07961-126704

Leicester Phoenix
Leicester Forest RUFC
Hinckley Road
Leicester Forest East
Leicester. 07799-072450

Manchester Knights
Medlock Leisure Centre
Garden Fold Avenue,
Droylsden, Manchester
07715-165422

Newcastle
Benfield Sports College
Benfield Road
Newcastle-upon-Tyne
07950-109372

North London Skolars
New River Stadium
White Hart Lane, Wood Green
London, N22 5QW
020-8889-1050

Nottingham Outlaws
Nottingham Moderns RUFC
Main Road, Wilford Village
Nottingham. 07773-612470

Oxford Cavaliers
North Hinksey Lane
North Hinksey Village
Oxford. 01865-510839

Rotherham Giants
Herringthorpe Stadium
Herringthorpe, Rotherham
07740-452638

South London Storm
Streatham & Croydon RUFC
159 Brigstock Road
Thornton Heath, Croydon
07818-290640

South Norfolk Saints
North Walsham Vikings RUFC
Norwich Road, Scottow
Norfolk, NR10 5BU
01603-538808

St. Albans Centurions
Old Verulamians RUFC
North Orbital Road
Cotlandswick, St. Albans.
07713-472091

Sunderland City
Newcastle Road
Fullwell, Sunderland
07901-864973

Teeside Steelers
Billingham RUFC
Greenwood, Billingham
Cleveland, TS23 4AY
07811-953390

West London Sharks
Grasshoppers RUFC,
Gillette Corner,
Twickenham
07711-105011

Wolverhampton Wizards
Wolverhampton RUFC
Castlecroft Road
Wolverhampton, WV3 8NA
07970-41074

Worcestershire Saints
Bromsgrove RUFC
Finstall Park, Finstall Road,
Bromsgrove, B60 3DH
07773-18833

Further information on the Rugby
League Conference from:
Julian Harrison
11, Herrick Way, Wigston
Harcourt, Leics., LE18 3LR.
Tel: 0116-266-1308. Fax: 0116-
266-0153. Mobile: 07885-546933

Rugby League Conference Grand Final: Crawley Jets versus
Rotherham Giants at Coventry RUFC, August 2000

Barrow Border Raiders: The Willie Horne Stand

Boundary Park, Oldham - the main stand

Australia: National Rugby League

Brisbane Broncos
Ground: ANZ Stadium, Kessells Road, Nathan, Brisbane
Headquarters: Fulcher Road, Red Hill QLD 4059
Post: As above
Telephone: +61 7 3858 9111
Fax: +61 7 3858 9112
Website:
http://broncos.131shop.com.au/index2.html *or* www.131shop.com.au
Email: media@broncos.co.au

Canberra Raiders
Ground: Bruce Stadium, Battye Street, Bruce ACT
Headquarters: 39 Torrens Street, Braddon ACT 2612
Post: PO Box 106, Braddon ACT 2612
Telephone: +61 2 6230 1711
Fax: +61 2 6230 5625
Website: raiders.com.au
Email: reception@raiders.com.au

Canterbury Bulldogs
Ground: Sydney Show*Ground*s, Homebush Bay
Headquarters: Edison Lane, (off Leylands Parade), Belmore NSW 2192
Post: PO Box 123, Belmore NSW 2192
Telephone: +61 2 9789 2922
Fax: +61 2 9718 8012
Website: bullbogs.com.au
Email: info@bulldogs.com.au

Cronulla Sharks
Ground: Toyota Stadium, Captain Cook Drive, Woolooware NSW 2192
Headquarters: As above
Post: PO Box 2219, Taren Point NSW 2229
Telephone: +61 2 9544 2311
Fax: +61 2 9544 1497
Website sharks.com.au
Email: sharks@sharks.co.au

Melbourne Storm
Ground: Olympic Park, Swan Street, Melbourne VIC 3004
Headquarters: As above
Post: PO Box 14714 Melbourne City Mail Centre, VIC 8001
Telephone: +61 3 9286 1100
Fax: +61 3 9286 7337
Website: melbournestorm.com.au
Email:
ashleyfree@melbournestorm.com.au

Newcastle Knights
Ground: Marathon Stadium, Turton Road, New Lambton
Headquarters: Level 3, 85 Hunter Street, Newcastle West NSW 2302
Post: PO Box 2191, Dangar NSW 2309
Telephone: +61 2 4927 6444
Fax: +61 2 4927 6555
Website: newcastleknights.com.au
Email:
knights@newcastleknights.com.au

New Zealand Warriors
Ground: Ericsson Stadium, Beasley Avenue, Auckland, New Zealand

Headquarters: 171-9 Beasley Avenue, Penrose, New Zealand
Post: PO Box 12777, Penrose, N.Z.
Telephone: 64-9-526-0888
Fax: 64-9-526-0889
Website: warriors.co.nz
Email: contact@warriors.co.nz

Northern Eagles
Ground: Brookvale Oval, North Power Stadium
Headquarters: 7-9 Federal Parade, Brookvale NSW 2100
Post: PO Box 1153, Brookvale NSW 2100
Telephone: +61 2 9905 3433
Fax: +61 2 9905 1764
Website: northerneagles.com.au
Email: info@northerneagles.com.au

North Queensland Cowboys
Ground: Dairy Farmers Stadium, Golf Links Drive, Kirwan QLD 4817
Headquarters: As above
Post: PO Box 577, Thuringowa Central QLD 4817
Telephone: +61 7 4773 0700
Fax: +61 7 4773 2595
Website: cowboys.com.au
Email: cowboys@cowboys.com.au

Parramatta Eels
Ground: Parramatta Stadium, O'Connell Street, Parramatta
Headquarters: 14 Ross Street, Parramatta NSW 2150
Post: PO Box 2666, North Parramatta NSW 1750
Telephone: +61 2 9683 6311
Fax: +61 2 9683 5587
Website: parraeels.com.au
Email: eels@parraeels.com.au

St George Illawarra Dragons
Ground: Sydney Football Stadium, WIN Stadium
Headquarters: (Sydney): 124 Princes Highway, Kogarah NSW 2217
(Wollongong): 1 Burelli Street, Wollongong NSW 2500
Post: (Sydney): As above
(Wollongong): PO Box 900, Wollongong NSW 2520
Telephone: (Sydney): +61 2 9587 1966
(Wollongong): +61 2 4225 8299
Fax: (Sydney): +61 2 9588 9039
(Wollongong): +61 2 4224 8790
Website: dragons.com.au
Email: dragon@dragons.com.au

Sydney Roosters
Ground: Sydney Football Stadium
Headquarters: 93-97 Spring Street, Bondi Junction NSW 2022
Post: PO Box 1532, Bondi Junction NSW 1355
Telephone: +61 2 9386 3248
Fax: +61 2 9387 3248
Website: sydneyroosters.com.au
Email: football@sydneyroostes.com.au

Wests Tigers
Ground: Leichhardt Oval, Campbelltown Oval
Headquarters: Level 1,14 Railway Parade, Burwood NSW
Post: PO Box 727, Burwood NSW 1805
Telephone: +61 2 8746 3200
Fax: +61 2 8746 3222
Website: weststigers.com.au
Email: jghosn@weststigers.com.au

French professional clubs

La Fédération Française de Rugby à XIII
30 Rue de l'échiquier.
75010 Paris
Tel: 33 1 48 00 92 56
Fax: 33 1 48 58 07 02

Albi
Stadium Municipal
81000 Albi
Siége social: 56, rue Porta
81000 Albi

Le Barcares
Hôtel de Ville B.P. 5
66420 Le Barcarès
Tel: 33 4 68 86 11 64

Cahors
Café Le Bordeaux
15 Boulevard Gambetta
46000 CAHORS
Tel. and Fax: 33 5 65 53 02 93

Carcassonne
29, Rue Victor Hugo
11 000 Carcassonne
Tel and fax: 33 4 68 47 74 74

Carpentras
Stade de la Roseraie
Route d'Orange
84200 Carpentras
Siége social: La brasserie le Van Gogh, Boulevard du Nord,
Carpentras
Tel: 33 4 90 60 38 38

XIII Catalan
Avenue des Sports
66000 Perpignan
Tel: 33 4 68 55 13 13

Chatillon
35, Avenue Clément Perrière
92320 Chatillon
Tel: 33 1 46 56 62 50

Entraigues
Place du 8 mai 1945
84320 Entraigues/La Sorgue
Tel: 33 4 90 83 63 92

Grand Avignon
"Les Bisons du Grand Avignon"
Parc des Sports
470 Avenue Pierre de Coubertin
84000 Avignon
Tel : 33 4 90 89 66 37
Fax: 33 4 90 88 60 81

Lezignan
Stade Le Moulin
Bd Claude Bernard
11200 Lezignan
Tel: 33 4 68 27 00 70

Limoux Rugby Xiii
33,Rue Petiet
11300 Limoux
Tel and Fax: 33 4 68 31 75 71

Lyon-Villeurbanne
80, Rue des Fontanières
69100 Villeurbanne
Tel: 33 4 78 68 08 58

Pia
Stade Daniel Ambert
Rue du stade
66360 Pia
Siége social: Salle des Moussous
Rue des Moussous, 66360 Pia

La Reole
Café du turon BP 97
33191 La Réole
Tel: 33 5 56 71 26 84

Roanne
56, Impasse Fontval
42300 Roanne
Tel: 33 4 77 72 76 99

RC Salon XIII
Siége: Rue du Capitaine Guibert
13300 Salon-de-Provence
Tel: 33 4 90 56 23 86 or
33 4 90 53 02 65
Permanence: Tous les jours
10 h - 12 h / 17 h - 19h30

St Cyprien
6, Rue Paul Eluard
66750 St Cyprien
Tel: 33 4 68 21 57 98

St Esteve-Roussillon
B.P. 15
66241 St Estève
Tel: 33 4 68 92 65 57

St Gaudens
Stade Jules Ribet
31800 St Gaudens
Club House et terrain d'entrainement
Stade du Saudet
Rue du Saudet
31800 St Gaudens
Tel: 33 5 61 94 44 40

Tonneins
"Le Robinson" BP 16
47400 Tonneins
Tel: 33 5 53 79 49 72

Toulouse
107, Avenue Frédéric Estèbe
31200 Toulouse
Tel: 33 5 61 57 80 00

Villefranche-Aveyron
Place Jean Jaurès
12200 Villefranche de Rouergue
Tel: 33 5 65 45 77 38

Villeneuve
Boulevard B. Palissey B.P. 107
47303 Villeneuve-sur-Lot
Tel: 33 5 53 70 08 28

Our thanks to
www.rugbytreize.com
for their permission to use the above information from their website. Click on to this site for all the latest news on French Rugby League. Information on the site is in French and English.

Rugby League Analysis, History & Vision

If you want to read about Rugby League in depth,
this is the magazine for you.

Published twice a year, it concentrates on the history of the game, and
analysis of current issues facing the game. It has a lively book review section
and a regular obituary section. Leading Rugby League writers contribute
regularly, including Robert Gate, Harry Edgar, Michael O'Hare,
Huw Richards and Phil Melling.

Order the latest issue for £2.00, or subscribe:

£7.00 for 4 issues   or

£10.00 for three issues plus a copy of one of the following books:
Tries in the Valleys - A history of Rugby League in Wales
From Fulham to Wembley - 20 years of Rugby League in London
The Fulham Dream - Rugby League comes to London

Order form: (Photocopy if you do not want to cut the book)
(Tick box)
Please send me the latest issue for £2.00   []
I would like a subscription:
£7.00 for 4 issues   []   £10.00 for 3 issues plus a book   []
Book chosen:

Name:

Address:

Phone:

Please send to: London League Publications Ltd, PO Box 10441, London E14
0SB. Cheques payable to London League Publications Ltd, no credit cards.

Rugby League books from London League Publications

Rugby's Class War
Bans, boot money and parliamentary battles
by David Hinchliffe M.P.
The story of League's battles with Union in parliament.
Published in November 2000 at £9.75. Special offer £9.00

From Fulham to Wembley
20 years of Rugby League in London
Edited by Dave Farrar and Peter Lush
A celebration of 20 years of professional rugby league in the capital.
Published in May 2000 at £8.75 Special offer £8.00

The Fulham Dream
Rugby League comes to London
by Harold Genders
The inside story of the creation of Fulham RLFC and the promotion winning
first season.
Published in September 2000 at £6.95. Special offer £6.00

London books special offer: **The above two titles for £12.00.**

Touch and Go
A History of Professional Rugby League in London
By Dave Farrar and Peter Lush with Michael O'Hare
Published in 1995 at £9.00. Special offer £5.00

Tries in the Valleys
A History of Rugby League in Wales
Edited by Peter Lush and Dave Farrar
Published in 1997 at £14.95. Special offer £8.00

All orders post free in UK, £1 per book overseas.
Order from: London League Publications Ltd., PO Box 10441,
London E14 0SB.
Cheques payable to London League Publications Ltd, no credit card orders.